MW00890862

SIE

Exam Prep 2024-2025

+699 FINRA Practice Q&As with Detailed Explanations for Securities Industry Essentials

By

Lincoln Kendrick

© **Copyright 2024 by Lincoln Kendrick - All rights reserved.**

This document aims to provide precise and dependable information regarding the covered topic and issue. The publication is sold with the understanding that the publisher is not obligated to offer accounting, officially permitted, or any other qualified services. If advice is required, particularly legal or professional, it is advisable to consult with a qualified individual in the relevant profession.

This declaration of principles has been accepted and approved by both a Committee of the American Bar Association and a Committee of Publishers and Associations. Any form of reproduction, duplication, or transmission of any part of this document, whether electronically or in print, is strictly prohibited. Recording this publication is also forbidden, and storage of this document is only allowed with written permission from the publisher. All rights are reserved.

The information presented herein is stated to be truthful and consistent. The recipient reader bears sole and complete responsibility for any negligence or misuse of the policies, processes, or directions contained within. Under no circumstances will the publisher be held legally responsible or liable for any damages, reparations, or financial losses resulting from the information provided herein, whether directly or indirectly.

The respective authors retain all copyrights not held by the publisher. The information in this document is offered solely for informational purposes and should be regarded as universal in nature. The presentation of information does not constitute a contract or any guaranteed assurance.

Any trademarks used in this document are without consent, and their publication does not imply permission or endorsement by the trademark owner. All trademarks and brands mentioned in this book are solely for clarification purposes and are the property of their respective owners, not affiliated with this document.

TABLE OF CONTENT

CHAPTER 1: INTRODUCTION TO THE SIE EXAM: STRUCTURE AND LATEST UPDATES

Embarking on the journey to understand and conquer the Securities Industry Essentials (SIE) exam is a pivotal step for anyone aiming to carve a niche in the financial sector. This chapter is dedicated to unraveling the structure of the SIE exam and bringing to light the most recent updates that candidates should be aware of.

Understanding the SIE Exam

The SIE exam serves as a foundational gateway for those aspiring to enter the securities industry. It is designed to assess a candidate's basic understanding of securities industry concepts, including the structure and function of the securities markets, the types of products and their risks, the regulatory agencies and their functions, and prohibited practices.

Exam Structure

- Types of Securities: This section delves into the characteristics, risks, and benefits of various financial instruments. Candidates are expected to differentiate between equity securities (stocks), debt securities (bonds), and derivative securities (options, futures). Understanding the nuances of these instruments, including how dividends, interest payments, and capital gains are generated, forms the bedrock of investment knowledge.

- Securities Markets: Here, the focus shifts to the mechanics of buying and selling securities. Candidates explore the roles of primary and secondary markets, the process of public offerings, and the intricacies of electronic trading systems. This section also covers the importance of market indices and the impact of market forces on securities pricing and trading volume.

- Regulatory Framework: A thorough understanding of the legal and regulatory environment is crucial for anyone entering the securities industry. This section covers the creation and enforcement of laws designed to protect investors and ensure market integrity. Key topics include the responsibilities and powers of regulatory bodies like the SEC and FINRA, the significance of the Securities Act of 1933 and the Securities Exchange Act of 1934, and the implementation of industry standards and practices.

- Prohibited Practices: Ethical conduct and adherence to legal standards are paramount in the securities industry. This section confronts the consequences of unethical behavior, including manipulation, insider trading, fraud, and other violations. Candidates learn about the mechanisms in place to detect and deter such practices, as well as the penalties imposed for violations.

Latest Updates

In an industry as dynamic as the securities sector, the SIE exam continually evolves to mirror the latest trends, regulatory changes, and technological advancements. This ensures that new entrants are well-versed in current practices and prepared to navigate the complexities of the financial markets.

Regulatory Changes

The regulatory landscape of the securities industry is subject to frequent changes, reflecting the need to address emerging challenges and ensure market integrity. Recent amendments and the introduction of new rules are pivotal areas of focus for the SIE exam. For instance, updates might include changes in compliance requirements for financial firms, adjustments in reporting standards, or the introduction of new investor protection laws. Understanding these changes is crucial, as they directly impact how businesses operate within the industry and how professionals advise and interact with clients.

Candidates should pay particular attention to updates related to the Dodd-Frank Wall Street Reform and Consumer Protection Act, the JOBS Act, and any amendments affecting the Sarbanes-Oxley Act. Additionally, new guidelines on anti-money laundering practices, cybersecurity measures, and ethical standards are also critical areas of study. These regulatory changes not only affect the day-to-day operations of financial institutions but also shape the broader landscape of the securities industry.

Market Developments

The SIE exam also incorporates updates on market developments to ensure candidates have a contemporary understanding of financial products and market practices. This includes the introduction of new investment vehicles, such as exchange-traded funds (ETFs), digital assets like cryptocurrencies, and environmental, social, and governance (ESG) investing criteria. As these products and practices gain prominence, understanding their mechanisms, risks, and regulatory considerations becomes essential for anyone entering the securities industry.

Moreover, the exam covers shifts in market dynamics, such as changes in trading volumes, market liquidity, and the impact of global economic events on financial markets. These topics are crucial for understanding how various factors influence market behavior and investment strategies.

Technology Impact

The increasing integration of technology in the securities industry has profound implications for market operations, regulatory compliance, and the nature of financial products available. Fintech innovations, including robo-advisors, blockchain technology, and the use of artificial intelligence in trading and risk management, are reshaping the industry. The SIE exam reflects these changes by incorporating questions on the impact of technology on the securities industry, emphasizing the importance of cybersecurity measures to protect sensitive client data and financial assets.

Candidates should familiarize themselves with the basics of these technologies and understand their implications for compliance, market integrity, and investor protection. This knowledge is not only vital for passing the exam but also for navigating a career in an industry increasingly dominated by technological advancements.

Enhancing Exam Preparedness

To excel in the SIE exam, candidates must not only memorize facts but also understand the application of these concepts in real-world scenarios. Active learning techniques, such as participating in simulation exercises and engaging with interactive study materials, can significantly enhance comprehension and retention. Additionally, candidates should focus on areas of recent regulatory changes and technological advancements, as these are likely to be emphasized in the exam.

CHAPTER 2: OVERVIEW OF REGULATORY FRAMEWORK IN THE SECURITIES INDUSTRY

The regulatory framework of the securities industry is designed to ensure transparency, fairness, and efficiency in the market. Understanding the roles and responsibilities of key regulatory bodies and the laws that govern the industry is essential for anyone looking to navigate the securities industry successfully. This knowledge not only prepares individuals for the SIE exam but also provides a foundation for ethical and compliant professional practice in the finance sector.

Key Regulatory Bodies

Securities and Exchange Commission (SEC): Established by the Securities Exchange Act of 1934, the SEC is the primary federal regulatory agency overseeing the securities industry. Its mission is to protect investors, maintain fair, orderly, and efficient markets, and facilitate capital formation. The SEC enforces federal securities laws, regulates securities exchanges, securities brokers and dealers, investment advisors, and mutual funds. The agency is also responsible for reviewing corporate filing requirements.

Financial Industry Regulatory Authority (FINRA): FINRA is a non-governmental organization that acts as a self-regulatory organization (SRO) for broker-dealers. Its role is to license and regulate broker-dealers, enforce rules governing the industry, and protect investors by ensuring the market operates fairly and honestly. FINRA oversees the activities of more than 4,500 brokerage firms and approximately 634,000 registered securities representatives.

Municipal Securities Rulemaking Board (MSRB): The MSRB regulates the municipal securities market. It establishes rules for securities firms and banks involved in underwriting, trading, and selling municipal securities—bonds issued by cities, states, and other local government entities. The MSRB's rules focus on protecting investors, municipal entities, and the public interest by promoting a fair and efficient municipal market.

Commodity Futures Trading Commission (CFTC): While not directly involved in the regulation of securities, the CFTC plays a crucial role in overseeing the U.S. derivatives markets, including futures, options, and swaps. Established by the Commodity Futures Trading Commission Act of 1974, the CFTC's mission is to foster open, transparent, competitive, and financially sound markets to avoid systemic risk and protect market users and the public from fraud, manipulation, and abusive practices related to derivatives and other products that fall within the CFTC's jurisdiction.

Office of the Comptroller of the Currency (OCC): The OCC charters, regulates, and supervises all national banks and federal savings associations as well as federal branches and agencies of foreign banks. While its primary role is to ensure that banks operate safely and soundly, it also oversees compliance with laws and regulations, including those that intersect with securities trading activities conducted by banks.

Key Laws and Regulations

Securities Act of 1933: Often referred to as the "truth in securities" law, the Securities Act of 1933 has two main objectives: to require that investors receive financial and other significant information concerning securities being offered for public sale; and to prohibit deceit, misrepresentations, and other fraud in the sale of securities. This act requires that any offer or sale of securities be registered with the SEC, unless an exemption applies.

Securities Exchange Act of 1934: This act created the SEC and granted it broad authority over all aspects of the securities industry. It includes provisions for the regulation of securities exchanges and market participants, as well as the prevention of market manipulation and insider trading. The act also mandates periodic reporting of information by companies with publicly traded securities.

Investment Advisers Act of 1940: This act regulates firms and individuals who advise clients on investment matters. It requires that all investment advisers working with portfolios of $110 million or more register with the SEC and adhere to regulations designed to protect investors, including rules regarding fees, personal trading activities, and fiduciary responsibilities.

Sarbanes-Oxley Act of 2002: Enacted in response to a series of high-profile corporate scandals, this act introduced major changes to the regulation of corporate governance and financial practice. It established new or enhanced standards for all U.S. public company boards, management, and public accounting firms. Key provisions include the requirement for CEOs and CFOs to certify the accuracy of financial statements and the creation of the Public Company Accounting Oversight Board (PCAOB) to oversee the audits of public companies.

Dodd-Frank Wall Street Reform and Consumer Protection Act: Enacted in response to the 2008 financial crisis, the Dodd-Frank Act represents one of the most significant changes to financial regulation in the United States since the regulatory reforms following the Great Depression. It aims to reduce systemic risk within the financial system, increase transparency, and protect consumers from abusive financial services practices. Key components of the Dodd-Frank Act include the Volcker Rule, which limits certain speculative investments by banks, and the creation of the Consumer Financial Protection Bureau (CFPB), which oversees financial products and services offered to consumers.

JOBS Act: Officially known as the Jumpstart Our Business Startups Act, this legislation was signed into law in 2012 to encourage funding of small businesses in the

United States by easing many of the country's securities regulations. It includes provisions that affect how companies can solicit investments and who can invest in startups, aiming to make capital more accessible to small businesses.

Regulation Best Interest (Reg BI): Implemented by the SEC in June 2020, Regulation Best Interest is designed to enhance the quality and transparency of retail investors' relationships with investment advisers and broker-dealers. It brings forth a new standard of conduct for broker-dealers, requiring them to act in the best interest of their retail customers when making a recommendation of any securities transaction or investment strategy.

CHAPTER 3: PARTICIPANTS IN THE SECURITIES MARKET AND THEIR ORGANIZATIONAL STRUCTURE

The securities market is made up of a wide range of participants, each contributing to the market's overall functionality and efficiency. From broker-dealers facilitating transactions to regulatory bodies ensuring market integrity, understanding the role of each participant is essential for anyone looking to make informed decisions in the securities industry. This knowledge not only aids in preparing for the SIE exam but also provides a solid foundation for a career in finance, offering insights into the intricate workings of the financial markets.

Broker-Dealers

Broker-dealers are pivotal in the securities market, acting as intermediaries that buy and sell securities for their accounts or on behalf of their clients. Brokers execute orders for clients, while dealers trade for their own accounts. These entities are essential for providing liquidity and facilitating the smooth operation of securities trading. They must register with the Securities and Exchange Commission (SEC) and are subject to regulation by the Financial Industry Regulatory Authority (FINRA).

Investment Advisers

Investment advisers offer advice about securities to clients and manage investment portfolios. They can be firms or individuals and are regulated by the SEC under the Investment Advisers Act of 1940. Advisers working with retail investors are now subject to Regulation Best Interest (Reg BI), ensuring they act in their clients' best interests.

Institutional Investors

Institutional investors, such as pension funds, mutual funds, and insurance companies, manage large pools of money and invest in securities, real estate, and other investment assets. They are significant players in the market due to the sheer volume of trades they execute, influencing market trends and pricing.

Individual Investors

Individual investors, or retail investors, participate in the market to meet personal financial goals, such as retirement savings, education funds, or wealth accumulation. They invest in stocks, bonds, mutual funds, and other securities, often relying on broker-dealers and investment advisers for transaction execution and investment advice.

Exchanges and Alternative Trading Systems

Securities exchanges, like the New York Stock Exchange (NYSE) and NASDAQ, provide marketplaces where stocks, bonds, and other securities are bought and sold. Alternative Trading Systems (ATS) offer trading platforms outside traditional exchanges, facilitating transactions in a more private setting. Both are crucial for maintaining market liquidity and price discovery.

Clearing Agencies

Clearing agencies ensure the proper settlement of securities transactions. They act as intermediaries between buying and selling parties to ensure the transfer of securities and cash. The Depository Trust & Clearing Corporation (DTCC) is a primary example, providing clearing and settlement services to the industry.

Regulatory Bodies

The SEC and FINRA are the primary regulatory bodies overseeing the securities market. The SEC enforces federal securities laws, while FINRA focuses on regulating brokerage firms and their registered representatives. Other regulatory participants include the Municipal Securities Rulemaking Board (MSRB), which oversees the municipal securities market, and the Commodity Futures Trading Commission (CFTC), which regulates commodity futures and options markets.

Transfer Agents and Registrars

Transfer Agents play a critical role in tracking the ownership changes of a company's stocks and bonds. They are responsible for issuing and canceling certificates to reflect changes in ownership and ensuring that investors receive the dividends and other benefits they are entitled to. Registrars work closely with transfer agents to ensure that a company's securities are not overissued and that the list of owners is accurate and up-to-date. These entities ensure the integrity of the company's securities, providing a crucial link between issuing companies and shareholders.

Credit Rating Agencies

Credit Rating Agencies, such as Standard & Poor's, Moody's, and Fitch Ratings, assess the creditworthiness of issuers of debt securities. They provide investors with an evaluation of the risks associated with debt securities, influencing interest rates and investment decisions. Their ratings range from high-grade (indicating low credit risk) to junk status (indicating high credit risk), affecting the cost of borrowing for issuers and investment choices for investors.

Custodians

Custodians are financial institutions that hold customers' securities for safekeeping to minimize the risk of their theft or loss. They can also offer other services, such as account administration, transaction settlements, collection of dividends and interest payments, and tax support. Institutional investors, such as mutual funds and pension funds, typically use custodians to safeguard their portfolios.

Market Makers

Market Makers are broker-dealers that accept the risk of holding a certain number of shares of a particular security to facilitate trading in that security. By quoting both a buy and a sell price in a financial instrument or commodity held in inventory, they provide liquidity and depth to the markets and ensure that trading is possible at any given time. Their role is crucial in enabling efficient market operations and providing continuous price quotations.

Government and Regulatory Advisors

Government entities, such as the Treasury Department and central banks, also play significant roles in the securities market. They issue government securities, implement monetary policies, and sometimes intervene in the financial markets to achieve economic stability. Regulatory advisors, including legal firms and consulting companies, assist market participants in navigating the complex regulatory environment, ensuring compliance and advising on the implications of regulatory changes.

CHAPTER 4: ECONOMIC INFLUENCES ON THE SECURITIES MARKET

The securities market does not operate in a vacuum; it is deeply influenced by a wide range of macroeconomic factors. Understanding these influences is essential for making informed investment decisions and anticipating market movements. By analyzing interest rates, inflation, GDP, unemployment rates, and the effects of fiscal and monetary policy, as well as global events, investors and financial professionals can better navigate the complexities of the securities market, aligning their strategies with broader economic trends for optimal outcomes.

Interest Rates

Interest rates, determined by the central bank in many countries, are among the most significant economic factors affecting the securities market. When the central bank raises interest rates, borrowing costs increase, which can slow economic growth and reduce corporate profits, leading to declines in stock prices. Conversely, lower interest rates decrease borrowing costs, potentially stimulating economic growth and boosting stock market performance. Interest rates also directly impact the bond market; as rates rise, existing bond prices typically fall, reflecting the higher yields offered by newly issued bonds.

Inflation

Inflation represents the rate at which the general level of prices for goods and services is rising, eroding purchasing power. Moderate inflation is often seen as a sign of a growing economy, but high inflation can lead to uncertainty and volatility in the securities market. Stocks may suffer in high inflation environments as companies face increased costs and consumers' purchasing power declines. However, certain assets like gold and real estate can act as hedges against inflation, attracting investors looking to protect their portfolios.

Gross Domestic Product (GDP)

GDP measures the total economic output of a country and is a key indicator of economic health. Rising GDP indicates economic growth, which can be positive for the stock market as companies benefit from increased consumer spending and investment. Conversely, declining GDP can signal economic trouble, potentially leading to decreased corporate earnings and lower stock prices. The bond market may react differently to GDP changes, as slower growth or recession can lead to lower interest rates and higher bond prices.

Unemployment Rate

The unemployment rate is a critical economic indicator reflecting the percentage of the labor force that is jobless and actively seeking employment. High unemployment rates can signal economic distress, potentially leading to decreased consumer spending and lower corporate profits, negatively impacting the stock market. Conversely, low unemployment rates indicate a strong economy, which can bolster market confidence and drive securities prices up.

Fiscal and Monetary Policy

Governments and central banks use fiscal and monetary policy tools to manage economic performance. Fiscal policy involves government spending and taxation decisions, which can influence economic activity and, by extension, the securities market. For example, increased government spending can stimulate economic growth, potentially boosting stock prices. Monetary policy, primarily concerning the management of interest rates and the money supply, directly affects the securities market through its impact on borrowing costs, consumer spending, and inflation.

Global Events

Global events, including geopolitical tensions, trade agreements, and international conflicts, can have profound effects on the securities market. Such events can introduce uncertainty and volatility, leading investors to seek safer assets like government bonds, impacting stock and bond prices worldwide. Additionally, global economic trends, such as emerging market growth or economic downturns in significant economies, can influence investment flows and securities market dynamics.

Currency Exchange Rates

Currency exchange rates play a pivotal role in the global securities market. Fluctuations in currency values can affect international trade balances, foreign investment flows, and the relative value of earnings for multinational corporations. A stronger currency can make a country's exports more expensive and less competitive abroad, potentially impacting companies' overseas earnings. Conversely, a weaker currency can boost exports by making them cheaper on the global market, potentially increasing corporate profits and positively affecting stock prices. For investors, changes in exchange rates can significantly impact the returns on investments denominated in foreign currencies.

Consumer Confidence and Spending

Consumer confidence is a key economic indicator that measures how optimistic or pessimistic consumers are about their financial prospects and the general state of the economy. High consumer confidence typically leads to increased consumer spending, which can drive economic growth and positively impact the securities market, particularly sectors reliant on consumer spending like retail, automotive, and real estate. Conversely, low consumer confidence can lead to decreased spending, slowing economic growth, and negatively impacting these sectors.

Technological Innovations

Technological advancements can have a profound impact on the securities market, influencing not only specific sectors such as technology and telecommunications but also the broader market landscape. Innovations can lead to new products and services, disrupt traditional industries, and create new investment opportunities. For example, the rise of fintech, blockchain, and artificial intelligence has introduced new ways of trading, new financial products, and increased market efficiency, all of which can affect market dynamics and investment strategies.

Environmental, Social, and Governance (ESG) Factors

The growing emphasis on ESG factors reflects a shift in how investors evaluate companies, with an increasing number considering the sustainability and ethical impact of their investments alongside traditional financial metrics. Companies with strong ESG profiles may be viewed as lower risk and more sustainable in the long term, attracting investment and potentially impacting their stock performance. Conversely, companies with poor ESG practices may face divestment and regulatory risks, affecting their market valuation.

Demographic Trends

Demographic changes, such as aging populations in developed countries or growing middle classes in emerging markets, can have significant long-term impacts on the securities market. These trends can influence economic growth, consumer spending patterns, and investment needs, affecting sectors such as healthcare, real estate, financial services, and consumer goods. Understanding these trends can help investors make informed decisions about long-term investment opportunities and risks.

CHAPTER 5: INITIAL AND SECONDARY OFFERINGS: A DETAILED LOOK

The processes and regulations surrounding initial and secondary offerings are foundational to the functioning of the securities industry. By understanding the detailed steps involved in an IPO and the dynamics of secondary market trading, individuals can better appreciate the complexities of the market and the regulatory efforts to maintain its integrity and fairness. This knowledge is not only vital for those preparing for the SIE exam but also for anyone looking to engage with the securities market, whether as a participant, investor, or professional.

Initial Public Offerings (IPOs)

An IPO marks a company's first sale of stock to the public, transitioning from a private entity to a public one. This process is pivotal for companies seeking to raise capital, expand their business, and enhance their public profile.

The IPO Process:

- Appointment of Underwriters: Companies initiate the IPO process by selecting underwriters, typically investment banks, to manage the offering. The underwriters conduct due diligence to evaluate the company's business, financial condition, and market potential.

- Registration Statement: The company files a registration statement with the Securities and Exchange Commission (SEC), including the prospectus, which provides detailed financial information, business operations, and risks involved. The SEC reviews the documents to ensure compliance with regulatory standards.

- Pricing: The initial price of the shares is determined based on the company's valuation, market conditions, and interest from potential investors. This step involves a roadshow, where the company and underwriters present to institutional investors to gauge interest.

- Going Public: Once the SEC approves the offering and the price is set, the company's shares are made available for purchase by the public on a securities exchange.

Underwriter Selection and Role Expansion:

The selection of underwriters is a strategic decision. Companies often choose underwriters based on their industry expertise, market reach, and previous IPO successes. The underwriters' role extends beyond initial evaluation and pricing; they also market the offering to potential investors, often through a syndicate of other banks to widen distribution. The underwriting syndicate collectively assumes the risk of buying the shares from the issuer and selling them to the public, sometimes guaranteeing a minimum price to the issuing company.

Due Diligence and the Roadshow:

The due diligence process is exhaustive, involving a thorough review of the company's financial performance, business model, management team, market opportunities, and risks. This phase is critical for setting the IPO price range, which is initially speculative and adjusted based on investor feedback during the roadshow. The roadshow itself is a marketing campaign where the company's executives and underwriters meet with institutional investors and analysts to sell the investment story, aiming to generate excitement and demand for the shares.

Quiet Period and IPO Pricing:

The "quiet period" is a regulatory requirement during which the company and its underwriters must limit public promotion of the company to prevent hype that could artificially inflate the stock price. Following the roadshow, the final IPO price is set based on investor interest, market conditions, and the company's valuation. This price determines the capital the company will raise and sets the stage for the public trading debut.

Post-IPO Considerations:

After going public, the company faces new challenges and opportunities. It must adhere to stricter regulatory requirements, including regular financial reporting and disclosure obligations. The company also gains access to capital markets for future financing needs but must now manage shareholder expectations and market reactions to its corporate strategies and performance.

Regulatory Considerations:

The SEC's regulatory framework ensures transparency and fairness in the IPO process. Key regulations include the Securities Act of 1933, which requires companies to disclose financial and other significant information through the prospectus, and the Sarbanes-Oxley Act of 2002, which imposes stringent requirements on financial reporting and corporate governance for public companies.

Secondary Market Trading

After the IPO, shares of the company are traded among investors on the secondary market. This market is essential for providing liquidity, allowing investors to buy and sell shares post-IPO.

Market Participants:

- Exchanges: Platforms like the New York Stock Exchange (NYSE) and NASDAQ, where securities are listed and traded.
- Broker-Dealers: Facilitate buying and selling securities on behalf of investors and may also trade for their own accounts.
- Investors: Range from individual retail investors to large institutional investors, all participating in the buying and selling of securities.

Regulatory Framework:

The secondary market is regulated to ensure fair and orderly trading and to protect investors. Key regulations include:

- Securities Exchange Act of 1934: Establishes rules for transactions on securities exchanges, requiring fair and transparent trading practices.
- Regulation NMS (National Market System): Aims to improve the efficiency of the secondary markets by enhancing competition among trading venues and ensuring that investors receive the best price executions for their trades.

- FINRA Rules: Govern broker-dealers' activities, ensuring they act in their customers' best interests and maintain market integrity.

Trading Venues and Mechanisms:

Secondary market trading occurs through various venues, including traditional exchanges and electronic trading platforms. These platforms use different mechanisms, such as auction-based systems on exchanges where buyers and sellers submit bids and offers, and dealer networks in over-the-counter (OTC) markets where dealers quote prices at which they will buy or sell securities.

Market Liquidity and Price Discovery:

Liquidity refers to the ease with which securities can be bought or sold in the market without affecting their price. High liquidity is characterized by a high volume of trading and tight bid-ask spreads. Price discovery is the process by which market prices adjust to reflect new information. It is a continuous process influenced by trading activity, news, economic indicators, and market sentiment.

Role of Market Makers and Specialists:

Market makers and specialists provide liquidity by maintaining inventories of stocks and quoting buy and sell prices. In exchange markets, specialists are responsible for facilitating trading in specific stocks, ensuring fair and orderly trading, and maintaining a book of public orders. Market makers in electronic and OTC markets quote prices for stocks and are ready to execute trades, benefiting from the spread between buy and sell prices.

Regulatory Updates and Compliance:

The regulatory landscape is continually evolving to address new market developments, technologies, and trading practices. Companies and market participants must stay abreast of changes to remain compliant. For example, recent updates have focused on enhancing transparency, protecting against market manipulation, and ensuring fair access to market data.

CHAPTER 6: FOUNDATIONS OF EQUITY SECURITIES

Understanding the foundations of equity securities is crucial for anyone entering the securities industry. Stocks represent not just a share of a company's assets and earnings but also a stake in its potential growth and success. Shareholder rights, including voting and dividends, are key aspects of stock ownership, while the equity market structure ensures a regulated environment for trading. This chapter lays the groundwork for deeper exploration into investment strategies, market analysis, and the role of equity securities in building diversified investment portfolios.

Basics of Stocks

Definition and Types:

Stocks are financial instruments that signify ownership in a company and represent a claim on part of the company's assets and earnings. There are two main types of stocks:

- Common Stocks: Common shareholders have the right to vote at shareholder meetings and to receive dividends, although these dividends are not guaranteed and can fluctuate.

- Preferred Stocks: Preferred shareholders typically do not have voting rights, but they have a higher claim on assets and earnings than common shareholders. Dividends for preferred stocks are generally fixed and paid out before dividends to common shareholders.

Issuance and Trading:

Companies issue stocks to raise capital for expansion, operations, or other corporate needs. Once issued, stocks are traded on stock exchanges, such as the New York Stock Exchange (NYSE) or NASDAQ, or through over-the-counter (OTC) markets. The price of a stock in the market is determined by supply and demand, influenced by the company's performance, investor sentiment, and market conditions.

Shareholder Rights

Voting Rights:

Common shareholders have the right to vote on corporate matters, including the election of the board of directors and significant corporate policies. Voting can occur at annual meetings or through proxy voting, allowing shareholders to vote without being physically present.

Dividends:

Shareholders may receive a portion of the company's earnings in the form of dividends. While preferred dividends are typically fixed, common dividends can vary based on the company's profitability and dividend policy.

Claim on Assets:

In the event of liquidation, shareholders have a claim on the company's assets after all debts and obligations to creditors have been satisfied. Preferred shareholders have priority over common shareholders in asset distribution.

Equity Market Structure

Exchanges and OTC Markets:

Equity securities are traded on regulated exchanges and in OTC markets. Exchanges provide a centralized, transparent platform for buying and selling stocks, with prices set by real-time supply and demand. OTC markets facilitate trades between parties directly or through dealer networks, often used for securities not listed on major exchanges.

Market Participants:

Participants in the equity market include individual investors, institutional investors (such as pension funds and mutual funds), and market professionals (such as brokers and dealers). Each plays a role in the liquidity and efficiency of the market.

Regulatory Environment:

The equity market is regulated by bodies like the Securities and Exchange Commission (SEC) in the United States, which oversees exchanges, market participants, and the issuance of securities to protect investors and maintain market integrity.

Stock Valuation Methods

Understanding how stocks are valued is crucial for investors. Several methods are employed to determine a stock's intrinsic value, including:

- Price-to-Earnings (P/E) Ratio: This common metric compares a company's share price to its earnings per share (EPS), providing insight into how much investors are willing to pay per dollar of earnings. A high P/E ratio might indicate that the stock is overvalued or that investors expect high growth rates in the future.

- Dividend Discount Model (DDM): This model values a stock based on the theory that its worth is equal to the sum of all its future dividend payments, discounted back to their present value. It's particularly useful for valuing companies that pay regular dividends.

- Discounted Cash Flow (DCF) Analysis: DCF analysis estimates the value of an investment based on its expected future cash flows, adjusted for the time value of money. This method is comprehensive but relies heavily on assumptions about future performance.

Stock Indices and Market Sentiment

Stock indices like the S&P 500, Dow Jones Industrial Average, and NASDAQ Composite provide snapshots of market trends and sentiment. They track the performance of a selection of stocks, representing various sectors of the economy, to gauge the overall health of the stock market and, by extension, the economy. Movements in these indices can influence individual stock prices and investor sentiment.

Impact of Economic Indicators

Beyond the direct financial performance of individual companies, broader economic indicators can significantly impact equity markets. These include:

- Consumer Price Index (CPI): Measures changes in the price level of a market basket of consumer goods and services, serving as a key indicator of inflation.
- Employment Data: Reports such as non-farm payrolls and unemployment rates can influence market expectations about consumer spending and economic health.
- Manufacturing Data: Indices like the Purchasing Managers' Index (PMI) provide insight into the manufacturing sector's health, affecting stocks in related industries.

Technological and Social Factors

The rise of algorithmic trading and social media has introduced new dynamics to equity markets. Algorithmic trading uses complex algorithms to execute trades at high speeds and volumes, potentially amplifying market movements. Meanwhile, social media can rapidly influence investor sentiment and stock prices, as seen in cases where stocks experience significant volatility due to trending topics or endorsements by influential figures.

Globalization of Equity Markets

The globalization of financial markets means that events in one part of the world can have immediate impacts on equity markets elsewhere. International trade agreements, geopolitical tensions, and global economic trends are increasingly relevant to investors in domestic markets. Diversification across geographies is a strategy used by investors to mitigate risks associated with any single market.

CHAPTER 7: PRIMER ON DEBT SECURITIES: BASICS AND TYPES

Debt securities play a vital role in the global financial markets, offering investors a mechanism for lending capital to a variety of issuers under terms that can meet a wide range of investment objectives. Understanding the basics of bonds, notes, and their characteristics is essential for anyone looking to navigate the debt markets, whether for personal investment, professional management, or preparation for the SIE exam. This chapter lays the groundwork for deeper exploration into debt investment strategies, risk assessment, and market analysis.

Introduction to Debt Securities

Debt securities are financial instruments through which governments, municipalities, corporations, and other entities raise capital by borrowing funds from investors. In exchange for lending their money, investors receive a promise of regular interest payments and the return of the principal amount, known as the face value, at maturity. Unlike equity securities, which confer ownership in a company, debt securities represent a loan from the investor to the issuer.

Characteristics of Debt Securities

- Principal: The face value of the debt security, which is repaid to the investor at maturity.
- Interest Rate: The rate at which interest is paid to the investor, which can be fixed, floating, or variable.
- Maturity: The length of time until the principal amount must be repaid, ranging from short-term (less than one year) to long-term (more than ten years).
- Issuer: The entity that issues the debt security, which can be a government, municipality, corporation, or other organization.
- Credit Risk: The risk that the issuer will default on its payment obligations. The creditworthiness of issuers is often assessed by credit rating agencies.

Types of Debt Securities

Government Bonds:

Issued by national governments, government bonds are considered among the safest investments, as they are backed by the issuing country's ability to tax its citizens and print currency. Examples include U.S. Treasury bonds, notes, and bills, which differ primarily in their maturities.

Municipal Bonds:

Issued by states, cities, and other municipal entities, municipal bonds finance public projects like schools, highways, and infrastructure. They come in two main types: general obligation bonds, backed by the issuer's credit and taxing power, and revenue bonds, supported by the revenue from a specific project or source.

Corporate Bonds:

Issued by corporations, these bonds typically offer higher yields than government and municipal bonds, reflecting the higher risk associated with corporate debt. Corporate bonds are categorized by their credit quality, from investment-grade (lower risk, lower yield) to high-yield or junk bonds (higher risk, higher yield).

Notes and Bills:

Shorter-term debt securities include notes (with maturities of one to ten years) and bills (with maturities of less than one year). These instruments are issued by governments and corporations to meet short-term financing needs.

Investing in Debt Securities

Investors choose debt securities for several reasons, including income generation through interest payments, preservation of capital, and diversification of investment portfolios. The selection of debt securities depends on the investor's risk tolerance, investment horizon, and income requirements.

Impact of Interest Rate Changes on Debt Securities

Interest rates have a profound effect on the valuation of debt securities. When interest rates rise, the prices of existing bonds typically fall, since new bonds are issued with higher yields to reflect the current rate environment, making existing bonds with lower interest rates less attractive. Conversely, when interest rates fall, the prices of existing bonds usually increase, as their higher interest payments become more desirable compared to new bonds issued at the lower rates. This inverse relationship between interest rates and bond prices is a fundamental principle of bond investing.

Role of Debt Securities in Risk Management

Debt securities can play a crucial role in the risk management strategies of both individual and institutional investors. By allocating a portion of an investment portfolio to bonds, especially those with high credit ratings, investors can reduce volatility and protect against the downside risk associated with more speculative investments. Furthermore, certain types of debt securities, such as Treasury Inflation-Protected Securities (TIPS), offer protection against inflation risk, preserving purchasing power over time.

Callable and Convertible Bonds

Beyond the basic types of debt securities, there are specialized forms like callable and convertible bonds that offer unique features and risks:

- Callable Bonds: These bonds give the issuer the right to redeem the bond before its maturity date, typically at a premium to the face value. Issuers may call bonds when interest rates decline, allowing them to refinance debt at lower rates. For investors, the risk is that bonds may be called away in declining rate environments, limiting their interest income potential.

- Convertible Bonds: Convertible bonds offer investors the option to convert their bonds into a predetermined number of shares of the issuer's common stock. This feature allows investors to participate in the upside potential of the company's equity while also enjoying the income and relative safety of a bond. The valuation of convertible bonds is influenced by both the bond market and the underlying stock's performance.

Emerging Trends in the Debt Market

The global debt market is continually evolving, with new trends emerging that reflect changes in investor preferences, regulatory landscapes, and economic conditions. For instance, the rise of green bonds, issued to fund environmentally friendly projects, highlights growing interest in sustainable investing. Additionally, the development of blockchain technology and its application in bond issuance and trading is beginning to transform market practices by enhancing transparency, efficiency, and security.

CHAPTER 8: ADVANCED DEBT INSTRUMENTS

Advanced debt instruments play a pivotal role in the financial markets, offering sophisticated mechanisms for financing, investing, and risk management. While they offer the potential for enhanced returns and strategic portfolio diversification, they also carry a higher level of complexity and risk. Mastery of these instruments demands a thorough understanding of their structures, market dynamics, and the economic and regulatory environments in which they operate. For professionals preparing for the SIE exam, a deep dive into these advanced debt instruments is not only crucial for exam success but also for navigating the complexities of the modern financial landscape.

Asset-Backed Securities (ABS)

Asset-backed securities are bonds or notes backed by financial assets. Typically, these assets consist of receivables like credit card payments, auto loans, and mortgages. The key feature of ABS is the pooling of assets into a financial structure that redistributes the cash flows from the underlying pool to investors in a prioritized fashion.

- Structure: ABS are structured into tranches, with each tranche offering a different level of risk and return. The senior tranches have priority in the cash flow from the underlying assets, making them less risky, while the junior tranches, which absorb losses first, offer higher yields to compensate for this increased risk.

- Market Dynamics: The ABS market is influenced by the performance of the underlying assets, changes in interest rates, and the overall economic environment. Investors need to assess the credit quality of the asset pool, the structure of the tranches, and the legal and financial safeguards in place.

Mortgage-Backed Securities (MBS)

Mortgage-backed securities are a type of asset-backed security secured by a mortgage or collection of mortgages. These securities are created when a number of these loans, usually with similar characteristics, are pooled together.

- Types: There are several types of MBS, including pass-throughs, where homeowners' payments pass from the original bank through a government agency or investment bank to investors, and collateralized mortgage obligations (CMOs), which are structured into multiple tranches with varying risk profiles.

- Interest Rate Sensitivity: MBS are particularly sensitive to changes in interest rates, which can affect the rate of mortgage prepayments. As interest rates fall, homeowners are more likely to refinance their mortgages, leading to early repayment of the principal on MBS and altering the investment's yield.

Collateralized Debt Obligations (CDOs)

Collateralized debt obligations are a type of structured asset-backed security (ABS) with multiple "tranches" that cater to a wide range of risk appetites. CDOs pool various debt instruments such as bonds and loans, and then issue new securities backed by the pool.

- Structure and Risks: The tranches in a CDO vary significantly in their risk profile and yield. The senior tranches are the least risky, while the equity tranches offer higher returns but bear the first losses. The complexity and risk of CDOs became particularly evident during the 2007-2008 financial crisis.

- Market Impact: The CDO market has undergone significant changes post-crisis, with increased regulatory scrutiny and demand for transparency. Despite this, CDOs remain a critical tool for risk distribution and investment diversification.

Municipal Derivatives

Municipal derivatives are complex financial instruments that municipalities use to manage interest rate risk, hedge against changes in the economic landscape, or speculate on future rate movements. These instruments can include swaps, options, and futures tied to municipal bond issuances.

Usage and Considerations: While municipal derivatives can offer significant benefits, such as cost savings and risk management, they also carry risks related to interest rate changes, counterparty risk, and market complexity. Understanding these instruments requires a deep knowledge of both the derivatives market and municipal finance.

Credit Default Swaps (CDS)

Credit default swaps are financial derivative contracts that allow an investor to swap or offset their credit risk with that of another investor. Essentially, a CDS provides insurance against the risk of default by a debtor.

- Functionality: In a CDS, the buyer of the swap makes payments to the swap seller up until the maturity date of the contract or until a credit event (such as a default) occurs. In return, the seller agrees to compensate the buyer if the debtor defaults on its obligations, effectively insuring the buyer against the risk of default.

- Market Impact: CDS play a crucial role in the financial markets by providing liquidity and enabling price discovery for credit risk. However, they also carry significant risks, as evidenced during the financial crisis of 2007-2008, when the opacity and complexity of CDS contracts contributed to systemic risk.

Inflation-Linked Bonds

Inflation-linked bonds, such as Treasury Inflation-Protected Securities (TIPS) in the United States, offer investors protection against inflation. The principal value of these bonds increases with inflation, providing investors with a return that is adjusted for changes in the purchasing power of money.

- Characteristics: The interest rate on inflation-linked bonds is typically lower than that on conventional bonds, reflecting the inflation protection they offer. However, their principal and interest payments adjust over time based on inflation rates, protecting investors against the eroding effects of inflation on fixed income investments.

- Strategic Importance: For investors seeking to preserve capital and maintain the real value of their investment income, inflation-linked bonds are an essential tool. They are particularly valuable in retirement portfolios and other long-term investment strategies focused on preserving purchasing power.

Sustainable and Green Finance

The rise of sustainable and green finance reflects a growing recognition of the importance of environmental, social, and governance (ESG) factors in investment decisions. Green bonds are a prominent example of this trend, offering a way for issuers to raise funds for environmentally friendly projects.

- Green Bonds: These bonds are specifically earmarked to be used for climate and environmental projects. They have gained popularity among investors looking to contribute to environmental sustainability while earning a return on their investment.

- Impact and Challenges: While green bonds represent a significant step toward aligning financial markets with environmental sustainability goals, challenges remain in terms of standardization, verification, and the measurement of environmental impact. Nonetheless, the market for green bonds and other ESG-focused financial instruments is rapidly expanding, driven by investor demand for sustainable investment options.

CHAPTER 9: STRUCTURED PRODUCTS AND PACKAGED INVESTMENT OPTIONS

Structured products, mutual funds, and ETFs offer investors a range of options to tailor their investment strategies according to their risk tolerance, financial goals, and market outlook. While structured products cater to those seeking customized solutions and risk management features, mutual funds and ETFs provide accessible, diversified investment vehicles suitable for a broad spectrum of investors. Understanding the nuances of these investment options, including their structures, costs, and potential benefits, is crucial for making informed decisions and effectively navigating the investment landscape.

Structured Products

Structured products are complex financial instruments created to meet specific investment strategies or risk profiles. They are typically constructed by packaging traditional securities with derivatives to offer protection against downside risk, enhanced returns, or both.

Characteristics: These products can be tailored to suit a wide range of market views and outcomes. They often include a principal protection component and might be linked to the performance of one or more underlying assets, such as stocks, indices, commodities, or interest rates.

Considerations: While structured products can offer attractive features, such as capital protection and potential for higher returns, they are complex and may carry high fees. Their performance is closely tied to the underlying asset or index, and they often have limited liquidity, making them suitable primarily for sophisticated investors.

Mutual Funds

Mutual funds pool money from many investors to purchase a diversified portfolio of stocks, bonds, or other securities. They offer an accessible way for individual investors to achieve diversification and professional management.

Types: There are various types of mutual funds, including equity funds, bond funds, balanced funds, and money market funds, each targeting different market segments and investment objectives.

Advantages: Mutual funds provide diversification, professional management, and liquidity. They allow investors to participate in a broad array of securities with a relatively small investment amount.

Fees and Expenses: Investors in mutual funds incur fees, which can include sales charges (loads) and annual expenses. The impact of these fees on investment returns varies by fund.

Exchange-Traded Funds (ETFs)

Exchange-traded funds combine features of mutual funds and stocks. Like mutual funds, ETFs hold a diversified portfolio of assets. However, they trade on stock exchanges at market-determined prices, similar to individual stocks.

Flexibility and Liquidity: ETFs offer intraday liquidity, allowing investors to buy and sell shares throughout the trading day at current market prices. This flexibility is one of the key advantages of ETFs over mutual funds, which are only priced at the end of the trading day.

Cost-Effectiveness: ETFs typically have lower expense ratios than mutual funds, partly because many ETFs are passively managed, tracking the performance of a specific index. However, actively managed ETFs and those targeting niche markets may have higher costs.

Tax Efficiency: ETFs are generally more tax-efficient than mutual funds due to their unique creation and redemption process, which helps minimize capital gains distributions.

Hedge Funds

Hedge funds are investment funds that employ diverse and often complex strategies to achieve returns for their investors. They are typically open to a limited range of accredited or institutional investors and are known for their flexibility in investment techniques.

- Strategies: Hedge fund strategies can include long-short equity, market neutral, global macro, event-driven, and many others. These strategies aim to generate alpha, or excess returns, regardless of market conditions.

- Considerations: Hedge funds often use leverage and derivatives to amplify their investment strategies, which can also increase risk. They are less regulated than mutual funds and ETFs, offering more flexibility but also potentially higher fees and less transparency.

Operational Structure of Hedge Funds

Hedge funds are structured to maximize investment flexibility, often organized as limited partnerships (LPs) or limited liability companies (LLCs). This structure allows the hedge fund manager, who acts as the general partner or managing member, to make investment decisions on behalf of the fund while limiting the liability of the investors, or limited partners.

- Lock-Up Periods: Many hedge funds require investors to commit their capital for a specified period, known as a lock-up period, during which withdrawals are restricted. This allows the fund to pursue long-term strategies without the need to maintain high levels of liquidity for redemptions.

- Side Pockets: Some hedge funds use side pockets for illiquid investments, segregating these assets from the main portfolio to manage redemption requests more effectively. This practice allows the fund to invest in opportunities that may take longer to realize a return without impacting the overall liquidity of the fund.

Investor Qualifications for Hedge Funds

Investing in hedge funds is typically reserved for accredited investors and institutions due to the complex and risky nature of their investment strategies. Accredited investors are defined by regulatory authorities based on income, net worth, and financial sophistication criteria.

- Accreditation Criteria: In the United States, accredited investors must meet specific income or net worth thresholds, such as an annual income exceeding $200,000 ($300,000 for joint income with a spouse) for the last two years or a net worth exceeding $1 million, excluding the value of the primary residence.
- Institutional Investors: Institutional investors, including pension funds, endowments, and foundations, often allocate a portion of their portfolios to hedge funds to achieve diversification and potentially higher returns. These entities are typically subject to different regulatory standards due to their size and sophistication.

The Evolving Landscape of Hedge Fund Investments

The hedge fund industry is continuously evolving, with changes in regulatory frameworks, investment strategies, and market dynamics shaping its future.

- Regulatory Changes: In response to the financial crisis and calls for greater transparency, the regulatory environment for hedge funds has evolved, with increased reporting requirements and oversight. These changes aim to protect investors and the financial system without stifling innovation.
- Emerging Strategies: Hedge funds are increasingly exploring new strategies and asset classes, including digital assets like cryptocurrencies, private equity, and venture capital investments. These areas offer new opportunities for growth but also present unique risks and challenges.
- Technological Advancements: Technology plays a significant role in the hedge fund industry, with advancements in data analytics, artificial intelligence, and machine learning enabling funds to identify investment opportunities, manage risks, and optimize portfolio performance more effectively.

Real Estate Investment Trusts (REITs)

REITs allow investors to participate in portfolios of real estate assets. They are companies that own, operate, or finance income-producing real estate across a range of property sectors.

Types: There are equity REITs, which own and manage real estate properties; mortgage REITs, which provide financing for real estate; and hybrid REITs, which combine both approaches.

Advantages: REITs offer investors exposure to real estate without the need to directly buy, manage, or finance properties. They are required to distribute at least 90% of their taxable income to shareholders as dividends, providing a potential income stream.

Market Dynamics: The performance of REITs is closely tied to the real estate market and can be influenced by factors such as interest rates, economic growth, and sector-specific trends.

Digital Asset Investments

The rise of blockchain technology has ushered in a new era of digital asset investments, including cryptocurrencies and tokenized assets.

Cryptocurrencies: Digital or virtual currencies that use cryptography for security and operate on decentralized blockchain technology. Bitcoin and Ethereum are among the most well-known, but there are thousands of cryptocurrencies with various functions and underlying technologies.

Tokenized Assets: Traditional assets, such as real estate, art, or commodities, can be represented as digital tokens on a blockchain, offering a new way to invest in and trade these assets with the benefits of transparency, security, and efficiency provided by blockchain technology.

Considerations: Digital asset investments are highly volatile and subject to evolving regulatory landscapes. While they offer the potential for high returns, they also carry significant risks, including market, regulatory, and technological risks.

CHAPTER 10: COMPREHENSIVE GUIDE TO VARIABLE ANNUITIES AND MUNICIPAL SECURITIES

Variable annuities and municipal securities represent key components of a diversified investment strategy, each offering distinct advantages and considerations. Variable annuities provide a combination of investment growth potential and income options with tax deferral benefits, making them a compelling choice for retirement planning. Municipal securities offer the allure of tax-advantaged income and the opportunity to invest in the betterment of public infrastructure and services. Understanding the complexities, costs, and benefits of these investment vehicles is crucial for investors seeking to optimize their portfolios and achieve their financial objectives.

Variable Annuities

Variable annuities are insurance contracts that allow investors to participate in the potential growth of the financial markets while providing options for income in retirement and death benefits. They are complex products that combine investment and insurance features.

- Investment Options: Policyholders can allocate their premiums among a range of investment options, typically mutual funds, which can vary in risk and return. The value of the annuity contract will fluctuate based on the performance of the selected investment options.

- Income Options: Variable annuities offer a variety of payout options, including lifetime income, which can provide a steady stream of payments regardless of market conditions. This feature can be particularly appealing for retirement planning.

- Tax Treatment: Contributions to variable annuities grow tax-deferred until withdrawal, offering a tax advantage, especially for long-term investors. However, withdrawals before the age of 59½ may be subject to a 10% penalty in addition to ordinary income tax.

- Fees and Charges: Variable annuities can have high fees, including mortality and expense charges, administrative fees, and charges for additional features, such as enhanced death benefits or guaranteed minimum income benefits. These fees can impact the overall return on investment.

Annuity Riders

Annuity riders are additional features or benefits that can be attached to a variable annuity contract, often for an extra fee. These riders enhance the contract's flexibility and can provide tailored solutions to specific financial needs or concerns.

- Guaranteed Minimum Withdrawal Benefit (GMWB): This rider guarantees the annuitant can withdraw a certain percentage of the total investment each year, regardless of the underlying investment performance. It offers income stability while allowing participation in potential market gains.
- Guaranteed Minimum Income Benefit (GMIB): The GMIB ensures that, regardless of market conditions, the annuitant has the option to convert the annuity into a stream of payments based on either the actual account value or a guaranteed minimum value.
- Guaranteed Minimum Death Benefit (GMDB): This rider provides a guaranteed death benefit to the annuitant's beneficiaries, which can be higher than the account value if the underlying investments perform poorly. It offers a form of life insurance protection within the annuity contract.

Estate Planning and Wealth Transfer

Variable annuities can also play a strategic role in estate planning and wealth transfer, offering mechanisms to efficiently pass wealth to heirs while providing potential tax advantages.

Tax-Deferred Growth: The tax-deferred growth feature of variable annuities can be particularly beneficial in estate planning, as it allows the investment to grow without current tax liability. This can result in a larger accumulation of assets to pass on to heirs.

Stretch Annuity Options: Some variable annuities offer "stretch" options, allowing beneficiaries to continue the tax-deferred status of the inherited annuity over their lifetimes. This can provide a long-term income stream while spreading out the tax implications of distributions.

Non-Probate Asset: Since variable annuities are contract-based, they typically bypass the probate process, allowing for direct transfer to beneficiaries. This can simplify the transfer of assets and potentially reduce the time and costs associated with probate.

Municipal Securities

Municipal securities, or "munis," are debt obligations issued by states, cities, counties, and other governmental entities to fund public projects like schools, highways, and infrastructure. They offer tax advantages and are popular among tax-sensitive investors.

Types of Municipal Bonds:

- General Obligation Bonds (GOs): Backed by the full faith and credit of the issuer, with repayment guaranteed by the issuer's taxing power.
- Revenue Bonds: Secured by specific revenue sources, such as tolls from a bridge or fees from a water treatment facility, rather than the issuer's general taxing power.

Tax Advantages: Interest income from municipal bonds is often exempt from federal income tax and, in some cases, state and local taxes, especially if the investor resides in the state where the bond was issued. This tax-exempt status can make munis an attractive investment, particularly for individuals in higher tax brackets.

Risk Considerations: While municipal bonds are generally considered to be lower risk, especially GO bonds, they are not without risk. Credit risk, interest rate risk, and liquidity risk can affect the performance and valuation of municipal securities. Additionally, changes in tax laws can impact the attractiveness of municipal bonds.

Credit Ratings and Municipal Bonds

Credit ratings play a crucial role in the municipal bond market, serving as a key indicator of the issuing entity's financial health and its ability to meet debt obligations. Ratings are provided by major credit rating agencies such as Moody's, Standard & Poor's, and Fitch Ratings, and they range from high-grade (indicating lower risk) to non-investment grade or junk (indicating higher risk).

- Impact on Investment Decisions: The credit rating of a municipal bond affects its attractiveness to investors. Higher-rated bonds generally offer lower yields, reflecting their lower risk, while lower-rated bonds offer higher yields to compensate for increased risk.
- Monitoring and Changes: Credit ratings are not static and can be upgraded or downgraded based on changes in the issuer's financial condition, economic factors, and other relevant considerations. Investors need to monitor these ratings and assess how changes might impact their investment portfolios.

Market Dynamics and Municipal Bond Pricing

The pricing and yields of municipal bonds are influenced by a variety of market dynamics, including interest rate movements, economic conditions, and supply and demand factors.

- Interest Rate Environment: As with other types of bonds, municipal securities are sensitive to changes in interest rates. Rising rates can lead to lower bond prices, while falling rates can increase prices.
- Supply and Demand: The issuance of new municipal bonds and investor demand for tax-exempt income can influence bond prices and yields. Significant new issuance can lead to lower prices, while strong demand can push prices higher.

Social Impact Bonds

An innovative development in the municipal securities market is the emergence of social impact bonds, also known as "pay for success" bonds. These instruments finance projects that aim to achieve specific social outcomes, with returns to investors contingent on the achievement of these outcomes.

- Structure and Goals: Social impact bonds are designed to fund initiatives in areas such as education, healthcare, and social services, with the goal of improving social outcomes and potentially reducing future public sector costs.
- Investor Considerations: While social impact bonds offer the opportunity to contribute to positive social change, they also carry unique risks, including the risk that the desired outcomes will not be achieved and investors will not receive their expected return.

CHAPTER 11: EXPLORING ALTERNATIVE INVESTMENT VEHICLES

Alternative investment vehicles like hedge funds and commodities offer sophisticated investors avenues for diversification, risk management, and potential returns uncorrelated with traditional equity and fixed-income investments. However, the complexity, higher risk, and often higher cost associated with these investments necessitate a thorough understanding and careful consideration. For those preparing for the SIE exam, a grasp of these alternative vehicles not only enriches their investment knowledge base but also equips them with the insights needed to navigate the broader financial landscape.

Commodities

Commodities represent a fundamental class of assets including natural resources and agricultural products, such as oil, natural gas, gold, silver, and grains. Investors can gain exposure to commodities through direct physical ownership, futures contracts, or commodity-focused funds.

- Market Dynamics: Commodity prices are influenced by a variety of factors, including supply and demand dynamics, geopolitical events, currency fluctuations, and changes in economic indicators. This can lead to significant price volatility, presenting both opportunities and risks for investors.

- Investment Vehicles: Direct investment in physical commodities is often impractical for individual investors due to storage and transportation challenges. Instead, many opt for commodity futures contracts, which allow investors to speculate on price movements without the need to physically hold the commodity. Alternatively, investors can choose commodity-focused ETFs and mutual funds, which provide diversified exposure without the complexities of futures trading.

- Role in Portfolio: Commodities are often viewed as a hedge against inflation and a means of portfolio diversification. Since commodity prices frequently move independently of stocks and bonds, they can provide a non-correlated asset class that potentially reduces overall portfolio risk.

Commodity Indices and Their Role

Commodity indices play a pivotal role in the investment landscape by providing benchmarks for the performance of commodity markets. These indices track the prices of a basket of commodities, offering investors a way to gauge overall market trends.

- Diversification and Exposure: Investors can gain exposure to a broad range of commodities through index-based products, such as exchange-traded funds (ETFs) that track commodity indices. This approach allows for diversification across different commodity sectors, including energy, metals, and agriculture, without the need for direct investment in physical commodities or individual futures contracts.

- Strategic Benchmarking: Commodity indices serve as benchmarks for portfolio performance and strategic allocation. By comparing the performance of their commodity investments against these indices, investors can make informed decisions about portfolio rebalancing and exposure adjustments.

Environmental and Sustainability Factors

The growing emphasis on environmental sustainability and ethical investing is increasingly influencing commodity markets. Investors are more conscious of the environmental impact of their investments and are seeking opportunities that align with sustainability goals.

- Green Commodities: Certain commodities, such as clean energy sources and sustainably produced agricultural products, are gaining attention from investors looking to support environmental sustainability through their investment choices.

- Sustainability Ratings: Similar to ESG ratings for companies, environmental and sustainability factors are becoming important considerations in the valuation of commodities. Commodities that are produced in an environmentally friendly and sustainable manner may attract a premium from socially conscious investors.

Digital Commodities and Blockchain Technology

The digital transformation of commodity markets is underway, with blockchain technology offering new ways to trade, track, and secure commodity transactions.

Tokenization of Physical Commodities: Blockchain technology enables the tokenization of physical commodities, allowing them to be traded as digital assets. This innovation can increase market efficiency, reduce transaction costs, and improve transparency by providing a secure and immutable record of ownership and transactions.

Smart Contracts for Commodity Trading: Smart contracts, self-executing contracts with the terms of the agreement directly written into code, are being used to automate and streamline commodity trading processes. This can facilitate faster settlements, enhance security, and reduce the potential for disputes.

CHAPTER 12: BASICS OF OPTIONS: AN INTRODUCTORY GUIDE

Options trading offers a rich array of strategies for investors, each with its own risk-reward profile. Understanding the basics of how options work, the terminology used, and the foundational strategies available is crucial for anyone looking to navigate the options market effectively. Whether for hedging, income generation, or speculative purposes, options can be a valuable addition to a well-rounded investment portfolio. Mastery of these concepts is not only essential for those preparing for the SIE exam but also for anyone aspiring to a career in the securities industry.

Understanding Options

Options are financial derivatives that give buyers the right, but not the obligation, to buy or sell an underlying asset at a predetermined price within a specific period. The two primary types of options are calls and puts.

- Call Options: Give the holder the right to buy the underlying asset at the strike price.
- Put Options: Grant the holder the right to sell the underlying asset at the strike price.

Options are characterized by their expiration date, after which the contract becomes void, and their strike price, which is the price at which the underlying asset can be bought or sold.

Option Pricing Models

Understanding how options are priced is crucial for traders and investors. The most renowned model for option pricing is the Black-Scholes model, which provides a theoretical estimate of the price of European-style options.

- Black-Scholes Model: This model calculates the option price based on several factors, including the underlying asset's current price, the option's strike price, the time to expiration, the risk-free rate, and the volatility of the underlying asset. It assumes a lognormal distribution of stock prices and continuous trading.

- Binomial Option Pricing Model: An alternative to the Black-Scholes model, the binomial model breaks down the option's life into a series of discrete time intervals and calculates the value at each point. This model is particularly useful for American options, which can be exercised at any time before expiration.

Understanding Option Moneyness

The concept of moneyness describes the intrinsic value of an option in its current state relative to the strike price of the underlying asset.

- Deep In the Money (ITM): Options that are far in the money have a high intrinsic value, making them more expensive but also less risky.

- At the Money (ATM): Options where the underlying asset's price is very close to the strike price have no intrinsic value but are sensitive to changes in the market.

- Deep Out of the Money (OTM): Options that are far out of the money have little to no intrinsic value, making them cheaper but with a higher risk of expiring worthless.

Open Interest and Volume in Options Trading

Open interest and volume are critical metrics that provide insights into the options market's liquidity and activity level.

- Open Interest: Represents the total number of outstanding option contracts that have not been settled. For each buyer of an option, there must be a seller, and each transaction contributes to the open interest. High open interest indicates a high level of liquidity, making it easier to enter or exit positions.

- Volume: Refers to the number of options contracts traded within a specific period. High trading volume often correlates with high liquidity and can indicate the strength of a price move or signal investor interest in a particular strike price or expiration date.

Options Terminology

- Premium: The price paid by the buyer to the seller (writer) of the option for the right to buy or sell the underlying asset.

- In the Money (ITM): Describes an option with intrinsic value. A call option is ITM when the underlying asset's price is above the strike price, while a put option is ITM when the underlying asset's price is below the strike price.

- Out of the Money (OTM): Refers to an option with no intrinsic value. A call option is OTM if the underlying asset's price is below the strike price, and a put option is OTM if the underlying asset's price is above the strike price.

- At the Money (ATM): An option whose strike price is equal to the current price of the underlying asset.

Exotic Options

Beyond the standard call and put options, the financial markets offer a variety of exotic options, which come with unique payoffs and conditions not found in more traditional options. These include:

- Barrier Options: These options become activated or extinguished when the underlying asset's price breaches a predetermined level. They are categorized into knock-in and knock-out options, depending on whether the barrier needs to be breached to activate or deactivate the option.

- Asian Options: The payoff of an Asian option is determined by the average price of the underlying asset over a certain period, rather than at a single point in time. This averaging feature reduces the impact of volatility on the option's price.

- Digital (Binary) Options: Digital options provide a fixed payoff if the underlying asset's price is above (for a call) or below (for a put) the strike price at expiration. The payoff is all or nothing, making the risk and reward profile straightforward.

Options Expiration Cycle

Options are subject to an expiration cycle, which determines when they expire. Understanding this cycle is crucial for managing positions and strategies effectively.

- Standard Expiration: For many equity options, this occurs on the third Friday of the expiration month. However, there are also weekly options that expire every Friday, providing traders with more flexibility and opportunities to trade around specific market events.
- Quarterly and LEAPS: Some options are available with quarterly expirations, and Long-term Equity AnticiPation Securities (LEAPS) may expire up to three years from their issuance, catering to long-term investment strategies.

Market-Neutral Strategies Using Options

Options offer unique opportunities for constructing market-neutral strategies, which aim to profit regardless of the direction of the overall market.

- Iron Condor: This strategy involves selling an out-of-the-money (OTM) put and buying a further OTM put, while also selling an OTM call and buying a further OTM call. The goal is to profit from the underlying asset's price remaining within a specific range, capturing the premiums received.
- Butterfly Spread: A butterfly spread involves buying one in-the-money (ITM) option, selling two at-the-money (ATM) options, and buying one out-of-the-money (OTM) option. This strategy profits from low volatility in the underlying asset, with maximum profit occurring if the asset's price at expiration is equal to the strike price of the options sold.

How Options Work

Options trading can serve various objectives, from hedging risk in a portfolio to speculating on future price movements of an asset. Here are some foundational strategies:

- Buying Calls: Investors buy call options when they anticipate that the price of the underlying asset will rise, aiming to profit from the increase while limiting potential losses to the premium paid.

- Buying Puts: Investors may buy put options to hedge against a potential decline in the value of owned assets or to speculate on the decline of an asset they do not own.

- Writing Options: The seller (writer) of an option earns the premium and assumes the obligation to buy or sell the underlying asset if the option is exercised. Writing options can generate income but comes with significant risk.

SPREAD STRATEGIES

Spread strategies involve simultaneously buying and selling options of the same type (calls or puts) on the same underlying asset but with different strike prices or expiration dates. These strategies are designed to limit risk while targeting specific price movements.

- Vertical Spreads: Involve options with the same expiration date but different strike prices. A bullish vertical spread (e.g., a bull call spread) involves buying a call option at a lower strike price and selling another call option at a higher strike price. Conversely, a bearish vertical spread (e.g., a bear put spread) involves buying a put option at a higher strike price and selling another put option at a lower strike price.

- Calendar Spreads: Involve options of the same strike price but with different expiration dates. They capitalize on differences in time decay rates between the short-term and longer-term options. For example, an investor might sell a short-term call option and buy a longer-term call option, betting on minimal movement in the underlying asset's price in the short term.

STRADDLES AND STRANGLES

Straddles and strangles are strategies used to profit from significant price movements in either direction, making them ideal for volatile markets where the direction of the move is uncertain.

- Straddle: Involves buying a call option and a put option with the same strike price and expiration date. If the underlying asset experiences a significant price movement in either direction, one of the options will become profitable enough to cover the cost of both options and potentially provide additional profit.
- Strangle: Similar to a straddle, but the call and put options have different strike prices. The call option has a higher strike price than the put option, making it a cheaper strategy than a straddle due to the lower initial premium cost. However, the underlying asset needs to move more significantly for the strategy to become profitable.

MANAGING RISK AND ENHANCING RETURNS

Advanced options strategies can be tailored to manage risk and enhance returns, but they require a thorough understanding of the underlying mechanics and market conditions.

- Adjusting Strategies: Traders can adjust their positions in response to market movements by rolling out (extending the expiration date), rolling up (increasing the strike price), or rolling down (decreasing the strike price) their options.
- Combining Strategies: Sophisticated investors might combine multiple strategies, such as using a butterfly spread in conjunction with a straddle, to capitalize on specific market forecasts or volatility expectations.

Options Trading Strategies

Beyond basic buying and selling, options can be combined into sophisticated strategies designed to achieve specific financial goals or manage risk.

- Covered Calls: Involves owning the underlying asset and selling call options against that holding. This strategy aims to generate income from the option premiums but limits the upside potential.

- Protective Puts: Involves buying put options for assets already owned, providing insurance against a decline in the asset's price.

- Spreads: Utilize combinations of buying and selling options on the same underlying asset with different strike prices or expiration dates to limit risk while targeting specific price ranges for profit.

Condor Strategy

The condor strategy is an advanced options trading strategy that involves holding four options contracts with different strike prices but with the same expiration date. It's designed to profit from a stock trading within a specific price range.

- Long Condor: Involves buying one in-the-money call, selling one lower high-in-the-money call, selling one lower out-of-the-money call, and buying one out-of-the-money call. This setup is used when the trader expects low volatility in the underlying asset.

- Short Condor: The inverse of the long condor, this strategy is utilized when a trader expects significant volatility but is unsure of the direction. It involves selling options in the middle strike prices and buying options at the outer strike prices to limit risk.

Iron Butterfly Strategy

The iron butterfly strategy is a combination of four different options contracts, aiming to profit from the underlying asset's price staying within a narrow range until expiration. It's a strategy that combines both risk and potential return in a balanced manner.

Setup: This strategy involves selling an at-the-money call and put, while simultaneously buying an out-of-the-money call and put. The sold options generate premium income, while the bought options protect against significant losses.

Use: The iron butterfly is best used when the trader has a neutral outlook on the market and expects low volatility. The maximum profit is achieved if the underlying asset's price at expiration is equal to the strike price of the options sold.

Synthetic Positions

Synthetic positions involve combining options to mimic the payoff of a traditional stock position. These strategies allow traders to replicate the economics of a stock position using options, often at a lower cost and with increased flexibility.

- Synthetic Long Stock: Created by buying a call option and selling a put option with the same strike price and expiration date. This position mimics the payoff of owning the underlying stock, benefiting from upward price movements.
- Synthetic Short Stock: Involves selling a call option and buying a put option with the same strike price and expiration date. This setup aims to profit from downward price movements, similar to short selling the underlying stock.

Option Greeks

Option Greeks measure the sensitivity of an option's price to various factors. They are crucial tools for traders to manage risk and make informed decisions.

- Delta: Measures the rate of change in an option's price with respect to a one-point change in the price of the underlying asset. It provides an estimate of the probability that an option will end up in the money by expiration.
- Gamma: Measures the rate of change in delta for a one-point change in the underlying asset's price. It indicates the stability of an option's delta, with higher gamma values suggesting greater volatility in delta.
- Theta: Represents the rate of change in an option's price with respect to time, essentially measuring the time decay of an option. As expiration approaches, theta increases, reflecting the loss of time value.
- Vega: Measures the sensitivity of an option's price to changes in the volatility of the underlying asset. A higher vega indicates that an option's price is more sensitive to volatility.

- Rho: Measures the sensitivity of an option's price to changes in interest rates, although it is generally less significant than the other Greeks for most traders.

Volatility in Options Pricing

Volatility is a key component in options pricing, reflecting the expected fluctuations in the price of the underlying asset. There are two main types of volatility:

Historical Volatility: Based on past price movements of the underlying asset, providing a measure of how much the asset has moved on average over a specific period.

Implied Volatility: Derived from the market price of the option itself, representing the market's expectation of future volatility. High implied volatility suggests that the market anticipates greater price movement, which can increase option premiums.

Options in Portfolio Management

Options can be strategically used in portfolio management to achieve various objectives, including income generation, hedging, and speculative gains.

- Income Generation: Strategies like writing covered calls can provide investors with an additional income stream while potentially enhancing the yield of an equity portfolio.
- Hedging: Options can be used to protect against downside risk in a portfolio. For example, protective puts can insure the value of a stock position against declines, acting as a form of portfolio insurance.
- Speculation: While speculative use of options carries higher risk, it allows for leveraging positions in the market with a limited initial investment. Traders can speculate on both the direction and volatility of the underlying asset.

CHAPTER 13: ANALYZING INVESTMENT RETURNS AND PERFORMANCE

Analyzing investment returns and performance is a multifaceted process that requires a thorough understanding of various metrics and methodologies. By mastering these concepts, investors can better assess the effectiveness of their investment strategies, make informed decisions, and adjust their portfolios to align with their financial objectives. This chapter equips readers with the essential knowledge to navigate the complexities of investment analysis, fostering a deeper understanding of how to measure and evaluate investment success.

Understanding Investment Returns

Investment returns are the gains or losses generated from an investment over a specific period. They can be expressed in absolute terms or as a percentage of the initial investment.

- Total Return: This encompasses all sources of return, including capital gains, dividends, and interest income, over the investment period. It provides a comprehensive view of an investment's performance.
- Annualized Return: To compare investments over different time periods, returns are often annualized, showing what the average yearly return would be over the investment period.

ADJUSTED RETURNS

Adjusted returns account for various factors that can affect the investor's actual gains or losses, providing a more accurate picture of an investment's performance.

- Inflation-Adjusted Returns: Also known as real returns, these are calculated by subtracting the inflation rate from the nominal return rate. This adjustment is crucial for understanding how much an investment actually grows in purchasing power.

- Tax-Adjusted Returns: Considering the impact of taxes on investment returns is essential, especially for investments in taxable accounts. Tax-adjusted returns reflect the after-tax gain or loss, depending on the investor's tax bracket and the nature of the investment income (e.g., long-term capital gains vs. ordinary income).

- Expense-Adjusted Returns: For investments in mutual funds or ETFs, the expense ratio can significantly impact returns. Expense-adjusted returns subtract the cost of owning the investment, such as management fees, from the total return, offering insight into the net performance.

THE POWER OF COMPOUNDING

Compounding is the process by which an investment earns interest not only on the principal amount but also on the accumulated interest from previous periods. This concept is fundamental to understanding how investments grow over time.

- Compound Annual Growth Rate (CAGR): CAGR provides a smoothed annual rate that describes the growth of an investment over a specific period as if it had grown at a steady rate. It's a useful measure for comparing the performance of different investments over the same period.

- Frequency of Compounding: The frequency with which interest is compounded—whether daily, monthly, quarterly, or annually—can have a significant impact on the effective return of an investment. More frequent compounding results in higher effective returns.

REAL VS. NOMINAL RETURNS

The distinction between real and nominal returns is vital for investors to understand the true value of their investment returns.

- Nominal Returns: Represent the raw return figures without any adjustments for inflation. They indicate the percentage by which an investment has grown in nominal terms over a period.

- Real Returns: Adjust the nominal returns for the effects of inflation, providing a clearer picture of the investment's growth in terms of purchasing power. Real returns are essential for long-term investors, as they reflect the actual increase in wealth.

Measuring Investment Performance

Several key metrics and ratios are used to measure and evaluate investment performance, each offering insights into different aspects of an investment's return profile.

- Risk-Adjusted Return: This measures how much return an investment has generated for each unit of risk taken. The Sharpe ratio is a common metric for assessing risk-adjusted returns, comparing the return of an investment to the risk-free rate, adjusted for the volatility of the investment.

- Benchmark Comparison: Comparing an investment's performance to a relevant benchmark, such as a market index, helps investors gauge how well the investment has performed relative to the broader market or a specific sector.

- Alpha and Beta: Alpha measures an investment's performance relative to a benchmark, representing the excess return of an investment relative to the return of the benchmark index. Beta measures the volatility of an investment compared to the market as a whole, indicating how much risk is involved with the investment.

SORTINO RATIO

The Sortino ratio refines the concept of the Sharpe ratio by differentiating harmful volatility from total overall volatility, focusing solely on the downside risk.

- Definition and Calculation: The Sortino ratio is calculated by taking the difference between the portfolio's return and the risk-free rate, divided by the standard deviation of negative asset returns, known as downside deviation. This metric is particularly useful for investors who are more concerned about the potential for losses in their portfolio than the overall volatility.
- Application: By concentrating on the downside risk, the Sortino ratio allows investors to assess the risk-adjusted return of an investment in a more nuanced way, especially for asymmetrical return distributions or strategies that aim to minimize losses.

TREYNOR RATIO

The Treynor ratio is another risk-adjusted performance metric that measures returns earned in excess of the risk-free rate per unit of market risk, using beta instead of volatility as the denominator.

- Significance: This ratio is particularly insightful for evaluating the performance of diversified portfolios or mutual funds, as it considers systemic risk, represented by beta. It provides a measure of how well an investment compensates the investor for taking on additional market risk.
- Interpretation: A higher Treynor ratio indicates a more favorable risk-adjusted performance, suggesting that the investment has generated greater returns per unit of market risk.

DRAWDOWNS

Understanding drawdowns is crucial for assessing the risk associated with an investment strategy. A drawdown measures the peak-to-trough decline during a specific recorded period of an investment, indicating the largest single drop from peak to bottom in the value of a portfolio.

- Risk Assessment: Analyzing drawdowns helps investors understand the potential for losses in their investments, providing a clear picture of the investment's volatility and risk profile over time.
- Recovery Analysis: Alongside the magnitude of drawdowns, the time taken for an investment to recover to its previous peak (recovery time) is also a critical factor. This can influence investment decisions, especially for those with a lower risk tolerance or a shorter investment horizon.

Evaluating Investment Strategies

Investment strategies should be evaluated not just on returns but also on how well they align with the investor's goals, risk tolerance, and investment horizon.

Diversification Effectiveness: Assessing how well a diversified portfolio has performed in reducing risk while aiming to maximize returns.

Cost Analysis: Evaluating the impact of costs, including management fees, transaction costs, and taxes, on investment returns. Lowering costs can significantly improve net returns over time.

Performance Attribution: Analyzing which factors contributed to the investment's performance, including asset allocation decisions, security selection, and market timing.

Time-Weighted Return (TWR)

The Time-Weighted Return is a method used to measure the compound rate of growth in a portfolio. This metric eliminates the distorting effects of inflows and outflows of money, providing a clear picture of the investment manager's performance.

- Calculation Method: TWR breaks down the investment period into sub-periods at each point of cash flow, calculating the returns for each sub-period and then geometrically linking them to measure the total performance.

- Application: TWR is particularly useful for evaluating the performance of fund managers or portfolios with frequent deposits or withdrawals, as it focuses solely on the investment decisions, not the timing of cash movements.

Money-Weighted Return (MWR)

In contrast to TWR, the Money-Weighted Return takes into account the timing and size of cash flows, making it sensitive to when investors add or withdraw funds. MWR is essentially the internal rate of return (IRR) on an investment.

- Significance: MWR provides insight into the actual return an investor has earned, influenced by both the performance of the underlying investments and the investor's decisions regarding contributions and withdrawals.
- Calculation Complexity: Determining MWR can be more complex than TWR, as it requires solving for the rate that sets the net present value of cash flows equal to zero.

Portfolio Rebalancing

Portfolio rebalancing is a critical aspect of investment strategy evaluation, ensuring that an investor's asset allocation remains aligned with their risk tolerance and investment objectives over time.

- Need for Rebalancing: Over time, market movements can cause an investor's portfolio to drift away from its target asset allocation, potentially exposing the investor to undesired levels of risk or opportunity cost.
- Rebalancing Strategies: Investors can rebalance their portfolios periodically by selling assets that have grown to constitute a larger portion of the portfolio than desired and buying assets that have shrunk below the target allocation. Alternatively, rebalancing can be triggered when an asset class's weight deviates by more than a set percentage from its target.

LIQUIDITY ANALYSIS

Liquidity refers to the ease with which an asset or security can be bought or sold in the market without affecting its price. Analyzing liquidity is crucial for understanding the risks and operational capabilities of an investment strategy.

- Market Liquidity: This aspect evaluates how quickly investments can be converted to cash, which is particularly important in times of market stress or when quick portfolio adjustments are needed.
- Liquidity Risk: Some investment strategies may involve assets with lower market liquidity, which could lead to higher costs or losses when attempting to exit positions. Understanding liquidity risk is vital for portfolio construction and risk management.

BEHAVIORAL FINANCE CONSIDERATIONS

Behavioral finance examines how psychological influences and cognitive biases affect the financial behaviors of investors and financial practitioners. Incorporating behavioral finance considerations into the evaluation of investment strategies can provide insights into potential pitfalls and areas for improvement.

- Overconfidence and Market Timing: Investors often overestimate their ability to predict market movements, leading to excessive trading and higher costs. Recognizing this bias can help in developing more disciplined investment strategies.
- Loss Aversion: The fear of losses can lead to suboptimal investment decisions, such as holding onto losing positions too long or selling winners too early. Strategies that incorporate rules-based selling or buying can mitigate the impact of loss aversion.

ESG INTEGRATION

The integration of Environmental, Social, and Governance (ESG) factors into investment analysis and decision-making processes has gained significant traction.

ESG considerations can impact investment returns and risk profiles, making them an essential component of strategy evaluation.

- ESG Performance Link: Research increasingly suggests that strong ESG practices can be linked to better financial performance and lower risk exposure, as they may indicate superior management quality and forward-thinking strategies.
- Investor Values and ESG: For many investors, incorporating ESG factors is also about aligning investments with personal values or societal goals, beyond financial returns. Evaluating how well an investment strategy incorporates ESG can be crucial for these investors.

CHAPTER 14: TRADING CONCEPTS: ORDERS, STRATEGIES, AND EXECUTION

Trading in the securities markets involves a complex interplay of order types, strategies, and execution practices. By mastering these concepts, traders can navigate the markets more effectively, making informed decisions that align with their investment goals and risk tolerance. This chapter lays the groundwork for understanding the essentials of trading, providing a solid foundation for those preparing for the SIE exam and a career in finance.

Understanding Order Types

The type of order placed can significantly impact the execution, timing, and price of a trade. Familiarity with the different order types is crucial for effective trading.

- Market Orders: These orders are executed immediately at the current market price. They are preferred for speed and certainty of execution but may be subject to slippage in fast-moving markets.

- Limit Orders: Limit orders specify a price limit at which the order can be executed. A buy limit order will only be executed at the limit price or lower, while a sell limit order will only execute at the limit price or higher. This control over price can prevent slippage but may delay or prevent execution if the market does not reach the specified price.

- Stop Orders: Stop orders become market orders once a specified price level is reached. They are often used to limit losses or protect profits on a position. A stop-loss order triggers a sale if the price falls below a certain level, while a stop-buy order triggers a purchase if the price rises above a certain level.

- Stop-Limit Orders: These orders combine the features of stop orders and limit orders. Once the stop price is reached, the order becomes a limit order, providing more control over the execution price.

- **Trailing Stop Orders:** These are a type of stop order that adjusts automatically as the market price of the asset moves in a favorable direction.

The order trails the market price by a specified distance (percentage or dollar amount), helping to protect gains while providing a safety net against significant losses.

- **Iceberg Orders:** Large orders that could impact the market price are often broken down into smaller, less conspicuous orders, known as "iceberg" orders. Only a portion of the total order is visible on the order book at any time, helping to minimize market impact.

- **Bracket Orders:** This order type involves the simultaneous placement of two opposite-side orders (a stop-loss and a take-profit order) to lock in profits and limit losses. Once one side of the bracket is executed, the other side is automatically cancelled, ensuring disciplined risk management.

EXECUTION NUANCES

- Execution Speed and Quality: Beyond the type of order, execution speed and quality are critical. Factors such as the choice of broker, the trading platform's efficiency, and the liquidity of the asset can all influence the speed and price at which an order is filled.

- Algorithmic Trading: Advanced traders and institutions often use algorithmic trading strategies to automate order execution based on predefined criteria. Algorithms can analyze market conditions in real-time and execute orders at optimal prices, often within milliseconds.

Strategic Applications of Order Types

- Multi-Leg Strategies: Options traders use complex multi-leg strategies, such as spreads, straddles, and strangles, requiring precise order types for each leg to manage risk and potential returns effectively.

- Event-Driven Trading: Traders focusing on event-driven strategies, such as earnings announcements or economic data releases, may use specific order types to capitalize on expected volatility. For example, a straddle might be set up using limit orders to enter positions just before the event.

Trading Strategies

Effective trading strategies are developed based on an investor's goals, risk tolerance, and market analysis. Here are some foundational strategies:

- Day Trading: Involves buying and selling securities within the same trading day, capitalizing on short-term price movements. Day traders require a good understanding of market trends and the ability to act quickly.

- Swing Trading: Targets gains in a stock within an overnight to several weeks timeframe. Swing traders utilize technical analysis to identify buying and selling opportunities in price trends and patterns.

- Position Trading: A longer-term strategy where traders hold positions for weeks, months, or even years, based on fundamental analysis and broader market trends.

Scalping

Scalping is a trading strategy that seeks to profit from very small price changes in securities. Scalpers aim to enter and exit trades within minutes, sometimes seconds, capturing gains on minor price movements.

- High Volume and Speed: Scalping involves making dozens or even hundreds of trades in a single day. Traders rely on high volumes and rapid execution to accumulate profits from small price changes.

- Market Analysis: Scalpers often use technical analysis, including order flow indicators and short-term chart patterns, to identify opportunities for quick entry and exit points.

Momentum Trading

Momentum trading involves buying securities that are showing an upward price trend and selling securities that are showing a downward trend. The strategy capitalizes on the continuation of existing market trends.

- Trend Identification: Momentum traders use technical indicators, such as moving averages, MACD (Moving Average Convergence Divergence), and RSI (Relative Strength Index), to identify securities with strong momentum.
- Risk Management: Given the reliance on trend continuation, momentum traders must be vigilant in their risk management practices, often setting strict stop-loss orders to protect against trend reversals.

Options Strategies for Trading

Options offer traders a versatile set of tools for speculation, hedging, and income generation. Beyond basic buying and selling of calls and puts, sophisticated options strategies can be employed for strategic advantage.

- Covered Calls for Income: Traders holding a long position in a stock can write (sell) call options against that position to generate income from the option premiums, a strategy particularly useful in sideways markets.
- Protective Puts for Hedging: Buying put options as a form of insurance on a held stock position allows traders to limit downside risk while participating in potential upside.
- Spreads for Limited Risk: Options spreads, such as credit spreads and debit spreads, allow traders to take directional bets on securities with defined risk and potential return. These strategies involve simultaneously buying and selling options of the same class but with different strike prices or expiration dates.

Execution and Market Mechanics

Understanding how trades are executed and the mechanics of the market is essential for successful trading.

- Bid-Ask Spread: The difference between the highest price a buyer is willing to pay (bid) and the lowest price a seller is willing to accept (ask). A narrower spread indicates higher liquidity.
- Market Depth: Refers to the market's ability to sustain relatively large market orders without impacting the price of the security. Depth is influenced by the

order book, which lists all buy and sell orders in the market for a particular security.

- Electronic Trading Platforms: The majority of trading is executed electronically, providing faster execution and greater transparency. Familiarity with electronic trading platforms is essential for modern traders.

Market Makers

Market makers are firms or individuals that actively quote two-sided markets in a security, providing bids and offers (ask prices) along with the market size of each. Their role is crucial in providing liquidity and depth to the market, ensuring that orders can be executed even in the absence of a direct buyer or seller match.

- Functionality: By continuously buying and selling securities, market makers facilitate smoother and more efficient market operations, reducing the bid-ask spread and improving market liquidity.
- Compensation: Market makers profit from the spread between the buying and selling prices of securities. They take on the risk of holding a certain amount of stock in their inventory to maintain a fluid market.

Dark Pools

Dark pools are private financial forums or exchanges for trading securities not accessible by the investing public. They allow institutional investors to trade large blocks of shares without exposing their intentions to the public market, minimizing market impact.

- Privacy and Reduced Impact: Dark pools provide a venue where large transactions do not influence the market price as significantly as they would in the public markets, protecting against price slippage.
- Controversy and Regulation: The lack of transparency in dark pools has raised concerns about market fairness and integrity, leading to increased scrutiny and regulation by financial authorities.

High-Frequency Trading (HFT)

High-frequency trading uses powerful computers and algorithms to execute a large number of orders at extremely high speeds. HFT firms exploit very small price discrepancies in securities across different markets or similar financial instruments.

- Market Efficiency: Proponents argue that HFT contributes to market liquidity and efficiency, narrowing bid-ask spreads and ensuring that prices reflect the most current market information.
- Criticism and Risk: Critics contend that HFT can lead to market instability, as seen in events like the Flash Crash of 2010. The debate continues over the balance between the benefits of HFT in terms of liquidity and efficiency versus the potential risks to market stability.

CHAPTER 15: THE PROCESS OF SETTLEMENT AND KEY CORPORATE ACTIONS

The settlement process and corporate actions are foundational elements of the securities industry, influencing the operational dynamics of trading and the strategic decisions of corporations. By mastering these concepts, individuals preparing for the SIE exam and pursuing careers in finance can better navigate the complexities of the market, make informed investment decisions, and advise clients with confidence. This chapter equips readers with the knowledge to understand the procedural and strategic aspects of securities trading and corporate governance.

Understanding the Settlement Process

The settlement process refers to the series of steps that are taken to complete a securities transaction after a trade is executed. This process ensures the transfer of securities from the seller to the buyer and the corresponding payment from the buyer to the seller.

- T+1, T+2, and T+3 Settlement Cycles: Settlement times can vary depending on the type of security being traded. For example, in the United States, most stock transactions settle on a T+2 basis, meaning the transaction is completed two business days after the trade date. Government securities and options may have different settlement cycles, such as T+1.

- Clearinghouses: These entities act as intermediaries between buyers and sellers to ensure the smooth completion of transactions. They take on the risk of the transaction, guaranteeing that sellers receive payment and buyers receive their purchased securities, which mitigates counterparty risk.

- Electronic Settlement Systems: Modern trading utilizes electronic systems, such as the Depository Trust & Clearing Corporation (DTCC) in the U.S., to streamline the settlement process. These systems enhance efficiency, reduce errors, and lower the costs associated with physical securities transfer.

Global Settlement Practices

While the T+2 settlement cycle is standard in the United States, settlement practices can vary significantly across global markets. For instance:

- Varied Settlement Cycles: Some markets operate on a T+1 settlement cycle, aiming for greater efficiency and reduced credit risk. Others may still use a T+3 cycle or have specific settlement periods for different types of securities.

- International Clearing and Settlement Systems: Cross-border transactions involve complex processes managed through international clearing and settlement systems, such as Euroclear and Clearstream. These systems facilitate the efficient transfer of securities and funds across countries, accommodating differences in time zones, currencies, and regulatory environments.

The Role of Custodians

Custodians are financial institutions that hold and safeguard an investor's securities to prevent them from being lost or stolen. Their role in the settlement process is critical, especially for institutional investors and those with significant, diversified portfolios.

- Safekeeping and Administration: Beyond holding securities, custodians also handle administrative tasks related to ownership, such as collecting dividends and interest payments, executing corporate actions, and providing transaction reporting.

- Risk Mitigation: By entrusting securities to a custodian, investors mitigate the risk of theft, loss, or damage to physical certificates. Custodians also ensure compliance with regulatory requirements for the safekeeping of assets.

Blockchain and Settlement

Blockchain technology presents a revolutionary approach to the settlement process, offering the potential for real-time (or near-real-time) settlement of transactions, thus significantly reducing settlement risk.

- Decentralized Ledger Technology: Blockchain operates as a decentralized ledger that records all transactions across a network of computers. This technology can automate and streamline the settlement process, making it faster, more secure, and less prone to errors.

- Smart Contracts: These are self-executing contracts with the terms of the agreement directly written into code. Smart contracts can automatically enforce and execute the terms of a trade upon meeting predefined conditions, further speeding up the settlement process.
- Pilot Programs and Adoption: Various financial institutions and market infrastructures are exploring or have already implemented blockchain-based systems for certain types of transactions. These pilot programs are testing the viability, security, and efficiency of blockchain in real-world settlement scenarios.

CHAPTER 16: MANAGEMENT OF CUSTOMER ACCOUNTS: PRINCIPLES AND PRACTICES

Effective management of customer accounts demands a comprehensive understanding of account types, fiduciary duties, ethical considerations, and regulatory compliance. By adhering to these principles and practices, financial professionals can build strong, trust-based relationships with their clients, providing them with the guidance and support needed to achieve their financial objectives. This chapter equips readers with the knowledge and skills necessary to navigate the complexities of customer account management, fostering a high standard of care and professionalism in the securities industry.

Establishing Customer Accounts

The process of opening and managing customer accounts involves several key steps, each designed to ensure that financial professionals can serve their clients' best interests while adhering to legal and regulatory standards.

- Account Registration: Involves collecting detailed information about the client, including identification, financial status, investment objectives, and risk tolerance. This information forms the basis for making suitable investment recommendations.

- Types of Accounts: Understanding the differences between individual, joint, trust, corporate, and retirement accounts is crucial for tailoring account management strategies to each client's specific needs and goals.

- Customer Agreements: These documents outline the terms and conditions of the brokerage relationship, including fees, services provided, and the rights and obligations of both parties. Clear communication and transparency in customer agreements are vital for establishing trust and managing expectations.

STRATEGIC CONSIDERATIONS FOR ACCOUNT SELECTION

Choosing the right type of account is a critical decision that can significantly impact a client's financial strategy and tax implications. Financial professionals must guide clients through this selection process with a strategic lens, considering factors such as:

- Tax Efficiency: Different account types offer varying tax benefits. For example, retirement accounts like IRAs or 401(k)s provide tax-deferred growth, while taxable accounts offer more flexibility but with potential tax liabilities on capital gains and dividends.

- Investment Horizon and Goals: The client's time horizon and financial goals should align with the type of account selected. Long-term goals such as retirement saving might be better suited to tax-advantaged accounts, while short-term goals may require the liquidity offered by taxable accounts.

- Legal and Estate Planning Considerations: Trust accounts and certain types of joint accounts can play a pivotal role in estate planning, offering mechanisms for asset transfer and protection that align with the client's broader legal and estate objectives.

ENHANCING CLIENT RELATIONSHIPS THROUGH COMMUNICATION AND DOCUMENTATION

Effective account management extends beyond the initial setup, requiring ongoing communication and meticulous documentation to adapt to clients' evolving needs and market conditions.

- Periodic Reviews and Adjustments: Regularly scheduled reviews of customer accounts allow financial professionals to adjust investment strategies based on changes in the client's financial situation, risk tolerance, or market dynamics. These reviews should be documented and communicated clearly to the client.

- Transparent Reporting: Providing clients with transparent, understandable reports on account performance, fees, and transactions is crucial for maintaining trust and ensuring clients are informed about their investments' progress.

LEVERAGING TECHNOLOGY IN ACCOUNT MANAGEMENT

Advancements in financial technology have transformed the management of customer accounts, offering tools and platforms that enhance efficiency, accuracy, and client engagement.

- Digital Platforms and Portals: Many financial institutions now offer online platforms that allow clients to view their account information, performance data, and financial analysis in real-time, fostering greater engagement and transparency.
- Robo-Advisors: For certain client segments, robo-advisors offer an automated, low-cost alternative for managing investments based on algorithms and predefined criteria. While not suitable for all clients, they can complement traditional advisory services for clients with straightforward investment needs.
- Cybersecurity Measures: With the increasing use of digital tools, ensuring the security of client data and transactions has become paramount. Financial professionals must prioritize cybersecurity measures to protect against unauthorized access and data breaches, maintaining the integrity and confidentiality of client information.

Fiduciary Responsibilities

A fiduciary duty is a legal or ethical relationship of trust between two or more parties. In the context of customer account management, financial professionals often have fiduciary responsibilities that require them to act in the best interests of their clients.

- Suitability vs. Fiduciary Duty: While all financial professionals must ensure that investment recommendations are suitable for their clients based on their financial situation and objectives, those with a fiduciary duty must take additional steps to put their clients' interests ahead of their own, including disclosing any potential conflicts of interest.

- Ongoing Monitoring and Review: Fiduciary responsibilities include not only making appropriate initial recommendations but also conducting regular reviews of customer accounts to ensure that investments remain aligned with clients' evolving needs and circumstances.

ETHICAL STANDARDS AND PROFESSIONAL CONDUCT

Fiduciary duties are underpinned by a set of ethical standards and professional conduct that go beyond mere compliance with laws and regulations. These standards demand:

- Transparency: Clear communication with clients about all aspects of the investment process, including potential risks, costs, and compensation received by advisors.
- Confidentiality: Safeguarding client information diligently, ensuring that personal and financial data are protected against unauthorized access and disclosure.
- Fairness: Ensuring that all clients are treated equitably, without favoritism or discrimination. This includes fair allocation of investment opportunities and transparent fee structures.

MANAGING CONFLICTS OF INTEREST

Conflicts of interest are inevitable in the financial services industry. Managing these conflicts in a way that protects clients' interests is a critical component of fiduciary responsibility.

- Disclosure: Proactively disclosing any conflicts of interest, including financial incentives that might influence recommendations, allows clients to make informed decisions about the advice they receive.

- Avoidance: Whenever possible, financial professionals should avoid situations that might lead to conflicts of interest. When avoidance is not possible, managing the conflict in the client's best interest is paramount.
- Compensation Structures: Aligning compensation structures with client outcomes can help mitigate conflicts of interest. Fee-based models, as opposed to commission-based models, can align financial advisors' interests more closely with those of their clients.

EVOLVING REGULATORY LANDSCAPE

The regulatory environment governing fiduciary responsibilities is continually evolving, reflecting changes in the financial markets, investment products, and consumer protection concerns.

- Global Perspectives: Different jurisdictions have varying standards and regulations related to fiduciary duties. Financial professionals working with international clients must navigate these complexities to ensure compliance and protect clients' interests.
- Regulatory Changes: In many regions, regulations are shifting towards stronger protection for investors, with increased emphasis on transparency, best interest standards, and the management of conflicts of interest. Staying abreast of these changes is crucial for financial professionals to maintain compliance and uphold fiduciary standards.
- Continuing Education: Engaging in continuing education and professional development helps financial professionals keep up with regulatory changes, emerging best practices, and innovative strategies for managing client accounts effectively.

Ethical Considerations and Compliance

Ethical considerations and compliance with regulations are foundational to the management of customer accounts. Financial professionals must navigate a complex landscape of laws and industry standards to maintain the integrity of their client relationships.

- Know Your Customer (KYC) and Anti-Money Laundering (AML): Regulations require thorough due diligence to verify the identity of clients and monitor transactions for suspicious activity. Compliance with these regulations is essential for preventing fraud and financial crimes.
- Privacy and Data Protection: Safeguarding clients' personal and financial information is not only a regulatory requirement but also a critical component of maintaining trust. Financial professionals must ensure that data is protected against unauthorized access and breaches.

INTEGRATION OF TECHNOLOGY IN COMPLIANCE PROCESSES

The use of technology has become increasingly critical in ensuring compliance with ethical standards and regulatory requirements. Financial institutions are leveraging advanced technologies to enhance their compliance frameworks:

- RegTech Solutions: Regulatory Technology (RegTech) solutions utilize advanced analytics, machine learning, and blockchain technology to streamline compliance processes, including KYC and AML monitoring. These tools can automate the detection of suspicious activities and improve the accuracy of client verification processes.
- Digital Onboarding: The digital onboarding of clients, facilitated by technology, can enhance the efficiency of collecting and verifying client information while ensuring compliance with KYC regulations. Digital platforms can also facilitate ongoing client engagement and education on compliance matters.

ESG CRITERIA IN CLIENT PORTFOLIO MANAGEMENT

As investors increasingly seek to align their investments with their values, the integration of ESG criteria into portfolio management has become a significant ethical consideration for financial professionals.

- ESG Compliance and Reporting: Financial advisors must be adept at incorporating ESG factors into investment analysis and decision-making processes. This includes understanding the regulatory landscape around ESG reporting and disclosure requirements, which are becoming more stringent globally.

- Client Alignment: Advisors must engage in thorough discussions with clients about their ESG preferences and objectives, ensuring that investment recommendations are not only financially sound but also align with clients' ethical and sustainability values.

EVOLVING LANDSCAPE OF DATA PRIVACY LAWS

With the increasing digitization of financial services, compliance with data privacy laws is paramount. The global landscape of data protection regulations is evolving, with significant implications for the management of customer accounts.

- General Data Protection Regulation (GDPR) and Beyond: In jurisdictions subject to GDPR, financial professionals must adhere to strict rules regarding the collection, processing, and storage of personal data. Similar regulations in other regions, such as the California Consumer Privacy Act (CCPA) in the United States, also impact how client information is handled.

- Data Breach Protocols: Compliance includes having robust protocols in place to respond to data breaches. This involves not only technical measures to secure data but also clear communication strategies to inform clients and regulatory bodies in the event of a breach.

CHAPTER 17: KEY COMPLIANCE ISSUES IN THE SECURITIES INDUSTRY

Compliance and ethical conduct are the bedrock upon which the securities industry is built. By understanding and adhering to the key compliance issues, regulatory frameworks, and ethical standards discussed in this chapter, professionals in the securities industry can contribute to the integrity, stability, and efficiency of financial markets. This commitment to compliance and ethics not only protects investors but also enhances the reputation and success of financial institutions and professionals.

Understanding Compliance in the Securities Industry

Compliance involves adhering to laws, regulations, and ethical standards established by regulatory bodies and governments to protect investors and ensure fair, transparent, and efficient markets. Key regulatory bodies include the Securities and Exchange Commission (SEC) in the United States, the Financial Conduct Authority (FCA) in the United Kingdom, and other international organizations that oversee securities markets globally.

- Regulatory Frameworks: The securities industry operates under a complex framework of regulations that cover every aspect of financial activities, from trading practices to disclosures, anti-money laundering (AML) efforts, and the prevention of insider trading.
- Ethical Standards: Beyond legal compliance, ethical standards guide the behavior of financial professionals, emphasizing honesty, integrity, transparency, and the prioritization of clients' interests.

ROLE OF TECHNOLOGY IN ENHANCING COMPLIANCE

The advent of regulatory technology (RegTech) has transformed the way firms approach compliance, offering tools that automate and enhance the efficiency of compliance processes.

Automated Compliance Monitoring: Advanced algorithms and machine learning models can continuously monitor transactions and communications for signs of non-compliant behavior, significantly reducing the risk of violations.

Enhanced Reporting Capabilities: RegTech solutions facilitate the aggregation and analysis of vast amounts of data, enabling firms to generate detailed compliance reports with greater accuracy and speed, aiding in transparency and regulatory oversight.

ESG CONSIDERATIONS IN COMPLIANCE

As investor interest in sustainable and responsible investing grows, ESG considerations have become integral to compliance frameworks. Firms are increasingly required to integrate ESG factors into their investment processes and disclosures.

- ESG Disclosure Requirements: Regulatory bodies worldwide are implementing rules that require firms to disclose how ESG factors are considered in investment decisions and the impact of investments on ESG objectives. This includes the EU's Sustainable Finance Disclosure Regulation (SFDR) and similar initiatives in other jurisdictions.
- Risk Management: Compliance with ESG considerations extends beyond disclosures to include the assessment and management of ESG-related risks, ensuring that firms are not only transparent about their ESG practices but also actively managing potential ESG risks in their portfolios.

GLOBAL REGULATORY HARMONIZATION EFFORTS

In an increasingly interconnected global financial market, efforts to harmonize regulatory standards across jurisdictions are crucial for reducing compliance complexity and fostering international cooperation.

- Cross-Border Regulatory Cooperation: International regulatory bodies, such as the International Organization of Securities Commissions (IOSCO), work towards aligning regulatory standards and practices to facilitate cross-border investment and enforcement cooperation.
- Impact of Global Standards on Local Compliance: Harmonization efforts can lead to the adoption of global best practices in local jurisdictions, raising the standard of compliance and investor protection worldwide. However, firms must navigate the nuances of local implementation of these global standards, requiring a deep understanding of both international and domestic regulatory landscapes.

Major Compliance Concerns

Several areas of compliance are particularly pertinent to securities industry professionals, including:

Insider Trading: One of the most critical areas of compliance involves preventing the misuse of material, non-public information for trading. Insider trading undermines market integrity and investor trust.

Market Manipulation: Practices such as spreading false information, executing wash trades, or engaging in pump-and-dump schemes are prohibited as they distort market prices and mislead investors.

Anti-Money Laundering (AML): Financial institutions must implement robust AML programs to detect and prevent the flow of illicit funds through the financial system. This includes customer due diligence (CDD) and suspicious activity reporting (SAR).

Client Onboarding and KYC: Know Your Customer (KYC) processes are critical for verifying the identity of clients, understanding their financial behaviors, and assessing the risk they pose in terms of money laundering or terrorist financing.

CYBERSECURITY THREATS AND COMPLIANCE

As the financial sector becomes increasingly digitized, cybersecurity emerges as a paramount concern. Regulatory bodies are intensifying their focus on how financial institutions protect sensitive client data and financial systems from cyber threats.

- Data Protection Regulations: Firms are required to adhere to stringent data protection standards, such as the General Data Protection Regulation (GDPR) in Europe, which mandates robust measures to safeguard personal data.
- Cybersecurity Frameworks: In response to growing cyber threats, regulatory agencies have developed comprehensive cybersecurity frameworks. Firms are expected to implement these frameworks to identify, protect against, respond to, and recover from cybersecurity incidents.
- Incident Reporting: Regulations often mandate the timely reporting of cybersecurity incidents to both regulators and affected clients, emphasizing transparency and accountability in the event of data breaches or cyber attacks.

SOCIAL MEDIA COMPLIANCE

The use of social media by financial professionals and firms presents unique compliance challenges, particularly concerning advertising, client communications, and the potential for insider information dissemination.

Social Media Policies: Firms must establish clear social media policies that comply with advertising regulations, prevent the sharing of non-public information, and ensure that all communications are appropriate and professional.

Monitoring and Archiving: To comply with record-keeping requirements, firms are increasingly adopting technologies that monitor and archive social media interactions involving their employees, ensuring that all communications can be reviewed for compliance.

CRYPTOCURRENCY COMPLIANCE CHALLENGES

The rise of cryptocurrencies and digital assets introduces new compliance challenges, as regulatory frameworks struggle to keep pace with the rapid innovation in this sector.

Regulatory Uncertainty: The classification of cryptocurrencies (as securities, commodities, or currencies) varies by jurisdiction, leading to a complex regulatory landscape that firms must navigate carefully.

AML and KYC for Crypto Transactions: Implementing AML and KYC processes for cryptocurrency transactions is particularly challenging due to the pseudonymous nature of blockchain technology. Firms must develop specialized processes to identify and report potentially suspicious activities.

Initial Coin Offerings (ICOs) and Token Sales: Firms involved in ICOs or token sales must navigate a patchwork of regulations concerning securities offerings, investor protections, and disclosures.

Ethical Standards and Best Practices

Upholding ethical standards is essential for maintaining the trust and confidence of investors and the public. Financial professionals must adhere to best practices that include:

Transparency and Disclosure: Providing clients with clear, accurate information about investment products, risks, and costs is fundamental to informed decision-making.

Conflict of Interest Management: Identifying and managing conflicts of interest, whether actual or potential, is crucial. This may involve disclosing conflicts to clients or taking steps to mitigate them.

Fair Treatment of Clients: Ensuring that all clients are treated fairly and equitably, without discrimination, and that investment advice is aligned with their goals and risk tolerance.

Navigating the Evolving Compliance Landscape

The regulatory and compliance landscape is continually evolving, driven by changes in technology, market practices, and emerging risks. Financial professionals must stay informed about regulatory changes, leveraging continuing education and professional development opportunities to remain compliant.

- Technological Advances: The rise of fintech and digital assets presents new compliance challenges and opportunities. Adapting compliance frameworks to address the risks and regulatory requirements associated with these innovations is essential.

- Global Compliance Considerations: For firms operating internationally, understanding and complying with the regulatory requirements of different jurisdictions is critical. This may involve navigating cross-border regulations and international sanctions.

GEOPOLITICAL SHIFTS AND COMPLIANCE

Geopolitical developments can have profound impacts on the regulatory environment, affecting international operations and compliance strategies for financial institutions.

Sanctions and Trade Agreements: Changes in international sanctions or trade agreements can alter the regulatory landscape overnight, necessitating quick adjustments to compliance protocols to ensure ongoing legal operations across borders.

Emerging Markets: As financial institutions expand into emerging markets, they encounter diverse regulatory environments. Navigating these requires a deep understanding of local laws and how they intersect with international compliance standards.

STANDARDIZATION OF GLOBAL COMPLIANCE PRACTICES

Efforts towards standardizing compliance practices globally aim to simplify the regulatory burden for international financial institutions and enhance the effectiveness of compliance programs.

International Regulatory Bodies: Organizations like the Financial Action Task Force (FATF) and the Basel Committee on Banking Supervision (BCBS) work towards harmonizing regulatory standards, particularly in areas like anti-money laundering (AML) and banking supervision.

Common Reporting Standards (CRS): The adoption of CRS for tax purposes is an example of how standardization efforts can aid in compliance, requiring financial institutions to collect and report information to their local tax authority, which then exchanges this information with tax authorities in other jurisdictions.

ETHICAL CONSIDERATIONS IN FINTECH INNOVATIONS

The rapid advancement of fintech poses unique ethical and compliance challenges, necessitating a forward-thinking approach to regulation and ethical considerations.

Algorithmic Bias and Fairness: As decision-making in financial services increasingly relies on algorithms, ensuring these algorithms are free from bias and operate fairly becomes a critical ethical concern. Regulatory frameworks are beginning to address these issues, focusing on transparency and accountability in algorithmic decision-making.

Privacy and Data Security in Fintech: The use of big data in fintech raises significant privacy concerns. Regulations like GDPR set a precedent, but the dynamic nature of fintech innovations requires ongoing vigilance and adaptation of privacy laws and data security measures.

Access and Inclusion: Fintech has the potential to enhance access to financial services for underserved populations. Ethical considerations include ensuring that these technologies do not exacerbate financial exclusion or lead to predatory practices.

CHAPTER 18: UNDERSTANDING AND AVOIDING PROHIBITED PRACTICES

Understanding and avoiding prohibited practices such as insider trading, market manipulation, and conflicts of interest is crucial for anyone working in the securities industry. By adhering to ethical standards and regulatory requirements, professionals can contribute to the integrity and efficiency of the markets, ensuring investor confidence and trust. This chapter provides the foundational knowledge necessary to navigate the complex landscape of prohibited practices, emphasizing the importance of ethical conduct and compliance in fostering a fair and transparent securities market.

Insider Trading

Insider trading involves trading a public company's stock or other securities based on material, non-public information about the company. This practice undermines market integrity and is strictly prohibited by securities regulators worldwide.

- Material Information: Information is considered material if it could influence an investor's decision to buy or sell the security. Examples include non-public earnings reports, news of a pending merger, or acquisition.
- Legal Ramifications: Individuals convicted of insider trading can face both civil and criminal penalties, including fines and imprisonment. The enforcement of insider trading laws is a top priority for regulatory bodies like the SEC.
- Preventive Measures: Companies often implement policies to prevent insider trading, such as "blackout periods" during which employees are prohibited from trading the company's securities ahead of earnings announcements or major corporate developments.

Detection of Insider Trading

The detection of insider trading has become increasingly sophisticated, leveraging technology and data analysis to identify irregular trading patterns and potential breaches of confidentiality.

- Surveillance Systems: Regulatory bodies and exchanges use advanced surveillance systems to monitor trading activity in real time, looking for patterns that may indicate insider trading, such as unusual trading volumes or price movements ahead of major announcements.
- Investigation Processes: Once suspicious activity is identified, a detailed investigation process is initiated. This may involve reviewing trading records, communications, and financial disclosures, and interviewing individuals involved in the trading activity.

Corporate Governance and Insider Trading

Effective corporate governance plays a crucial role in preventing insider trading. Companies are expected to establish robust internal controls and policies to manage the flow of sensitive information and ensure compliance with insider trading laws.

- Insider Trading Policies: Many companies adopt comprehensive insider trading policies that outline restrictions on trading company securities, procedures for handling confidential information, and guidelines for pre-clearing trades by insiders.
- Education and Training: Corporations often conduct regular training sessions for employees and insiders to educate them about the legal obligations and company policies related to insider trading, emphasizing the importance of ethical conduct and legal compliance.

Ethical Implications for Securities Professionals

The ethical implications of insider trading extend beyond legal compliance. Securities professionals must navigate ethical dilemmas and uphold the highest standards of integrity to maintain investor trust and market integrity.

- Ethical Decision-Making: Professionals must exercise sound ethical judgment when in possession of material non-public information, recognizing the broader impact of their actions on market fairness and investor confidence.
- Whistleblowing Mechanisms: Encouraging a culture of transparency and accountability, many organizations implement whistleblowing mechanisms that allow employees to report unethical or illegal activities, including insider trading, without fear of retaliation.

Market Manipulation

Market manipulation refers to attempts to interfere with the free and fair operation of the securities markets, creating artificial, false, or misleading appearances with respect to the price of, or market for, a security.

- Types of Market Manipulation: Practices include "pump and dump" schemes, where perpetrators inflate the price of a stock through false and misleading positive statements and then sell off their holdings at the inflated price; and "spoofing," placing orders with the intent to cancel before execution to manipulate prices.
- Detection and Enforcement: Regulatory authorities use sophisticated surveillance systems to detect signs of market manipulation, relying on market data analysis and whistleblower tips to investigate suspicious activities.

Additional Manipulative Practices

Beyond "pump and dump" schemes and "spoofing," the securities industry faces a variety of manipulative tactics, including:

- Layering: Similar to spoofing, layering involves placing multiple, non-genuine orders to create a false impression of demand or supply, influencing other traders to act on these misleading cues.

- Quote Stuffing: Involves placing a large number of orders and then canceling them almost immediately, aiming to overload the system and slow down other traders, thereby gaining an unfair advantage.
- Cornering the Market: This occurs when an individual or group acquires enough shares of a particular security to gain control over its price, subsequently manipulating it to their advantage.

Challenges in Regulating Market Manipulation

Regulating market manipulation presents several challenges, including the sophistication of manipulative tactics and the global nature of financial markets.

- Evolving Tactics: As technology advances, so do the methods of manipulation, often outpacing regulatory frameworks and detection methodologies.
- Cross-Jurisdictional Activities: Manipulative practices that span multiple jurisdictions complicate regulatory enforcement due to differing laws and the challenge of coordinating across regulatory bodies.

Evolving Strategies to Combat Market Manipulation

Regulators and financial institutions continuously develop strategies to detect and prevent market manipulation, leveraging technology and international cooperation.

- Advanced Analytical Tools: The use of AI and machine learning in surveillance systems allows for the analysis of vast quantities of trade data in real time, helping to identify patterns indicative of manipulative practices.
- Global Regulatory Cooperation: International regulatory bodies are increasingly collaborating to share information and strategies for combating market manipulation, recognizing that a coordinated approach is essential in a globalized financial market.
- Education and Awareness: Regulators and financial institutions are also focusing on educating investors and professionals about the signs of market manipulation, empowering them to recognize and report suspicious activities.

Conflicts of Interest

Conflicts of interest arise when a financial professional's personal or financial interests could potentially interfere with the duty owed to clients or the employer.

- Disclosure and Management: The key to managing conflicts of interest is through full disclosure to clients and taking steps to ensure that such conflicts do not compromise the advice or services provided.
- Fiduciary Duty: Certain financial professionals, such as registered investment advisors, are fiduciaries and have a legal obligation to put their clients' interests ahead of their own, including disclosing any conflicts of interest that might affect their recommendations.

Multifaceted Nature of Conflicts of Interest

Conflicts of interest can manifest in various forms, not only in the straightforward scenarios of financial gain but also in more subtle ways that may affect decision-making.

Soft Dollar Arrangements: These involve using client brokerage commissions to obtain research or other services. While potentially beneficial, they can create conflicts if not used solely for the client's advantage.

Cross-Selling Practices: Financial institutions offering a range of services might face conflicts when incentivizing professionals to cross-sell products, potentially leading to recommendations that are not in the client's best interest.

Strategies for Conflict Resolution

Addressing conflicts of interest requires a comprehensive approach, combining policy, culture, and technology to ensure ethical conduct and client-centric service.

Ethical Decision-Making Frameworks: Implementing frameworks that guide professionals through ethical decision-making can help in identifying and resolving conflicts of interest. These frameworks often involve a series of questions that prompt consideration of the client's best interest and regulatory obligations.

Client Consent: In situations where conflicts cannot be entirely avoided, obtaining informed consent from clients after full disclosure can be a viable approach to managing these conflicts, provided the client fully understands the implications.

Technology's Role in Managing Conflicts

Advancements in technology offer new tools for identifying and managing conflicts of interest, enhancing transparency and compliance.

Conflict of Interest Registries: Utilizing internal registries powered by database technologies can help track and manage potential conflicts, ensuring that all relevant information is considered in decision-making processes.

Analytics and Monitoring Tools: Big data analytics and monitoring tools can scrutinize transactions and behaviors for signs of conflicts, flagging issues for further investigation and ensuring compliance with internal policies and regulatory standards.

Cultural and Organizational Factors

The culture within a financial institution plays a critical role in how conflicts of interest are perceived and managed.

Culture of Integrity: Cultivating a culture that prioritizes ethical behavior and transparency can reduce the occurrence of conflicts of interest. Leadership plays a crucial role in setting the tone for the organization's ethical standards.

Training and Awareness Programs: Regular training on ethics and compliance can heighten awareness among professionals about the importance of identifying and properly managing conflicts of interest, reinforcing the organization's commitment to ethical practices.

Ethical Practices and Compliance Programs

To avoid prohibited practices, firms in the securities industry implement comprehensive compliance programs that include:

- Education and Training: Regular training sessions for employees on ethical behavior, regulatory compliance, and the identification and management of conflicts of interest.
- Surveillance and Monitoring: Continuous monitoring of trading activities and communications to detect and prevent unethical or non-compliant behavior.
- Whistleblower Policies: Encouraging employees to report violations of laws, rules, or company policies without fear of retaliation, often through anonymous reporting channels.

21. SIE EXAM PREPARATION: PRACTICE QUESTIONS AND ANSWERS

Understanding Products and Their Risks (175 Questions)

EQUITIES

1. What is a common characteristic of preferred stock?

A) Voting rights in company decisions

B) Higher claim on assets and earnings than common stock

C) Equal dividend payments to common stock

D) Unlimited growth potential

2. A stock split is most likely to:

A) Increase the company's market capitalization

B) Decrease the dividend yield

C) Increase the share price immediately

D) Increase the number of shares outstanding

3. Blue-chip stocks are:

A) Highly speculative stocks with high volatility

B) Stocks of large, well-established companies known for their stability

C) Stocks that pay no dividends

D) New issues with high growth potential

4. Growth stocks are characterized by:

A) High dividend yields

B) Rapid growth in revenue and earnings

C) Stability and predictability

D) Low P/E ratios

5. Which of the following best describes market capitalization?

A) The total dividends paid out in a year

B) The total assets minus total liabilities of a company

C) The total value of a company's outstanding shares

D) The total value of a company's debt

6. What does liquidity in the stock market refer to?

A) The ease of converting stocks into cash without affecting the stock price

B) The volume of stocks traded in a day

C) The amount of liquid assets a company holds

D) The stability of a stock's price over time

7. The term "bear market" signifies:

A) A market in decline, with stock prices falling 20% or more from recent highs

B) A market showing rapid growth and increasing stock prices

C) A stable market with little movement in stock prices

D) A market with high liquidity and volume

8. A company's P/E ratio is used to:

A) Measure its operational efficiency

B) Assess its share price relative to earnings per share

C) Determine its overall debt levels

D) Evaluate its dividend payout ratio

9. Dividend yield is calculated by:

A) Dividing the annual dividends per share by the stock's price per share

B) Multiplying the stock's price per share by the annual dividends

C) Dividing the stock's price per share by the annual dividends per share

D) Adding the annual dividends per share to the stock's price per share

10. What is an Initial Public Offering (IPO)?

A) When a company offers stocks to the public for the first time

B) When a company's stock is delisted from an exchange

C) A secondary offering of stocks

D) The annual meeting where shareholders vote on company issues

11. Insider trading involves:

A) Trading based on public information

B) Trading by anyone outside the company

C) Trading based on material non-public information

D) Short selling by company executives

12. A limit order is:

A) An order to buy or sell a stock at its current market price

B) An order to buy or sell a stock at a specified price or better

C) An order that becomes effective only if the stock reaches a certain price

D) An order to sell a stock at the market price once it falls to a certain level

13. Earnings per share (EPS) is:

A) The total market value of a company's shares

B) The amount of company profit allocated to each share of stock

C) A measure of a company's financial performance based on dividends

D) The total earnings divided by the price per share

14. A stock's beta measures:

A) The stock's dividend yield

B) The stock's volatility in relation to the overall market

C) The company's market capitalization

D) The liquidity of the stock

15. What does a high P/E ratio suggest about a stock?

A) The stock is potentially undervalued

B) The stock is likely overvalued or expected to have high growth

C) The company is experiencing financial difficulties

D) The stock has a high dividend yield

16. Short selling a stock implies that the investor:

A) Expects the stock price to increase

B) Expects the stock price to decrease

C) Owns the stock and is selling it

D) Is buying the stock on margin

17. The ex-dividend date is important because:

A) It is the date when the company pays out dividends

B) It is the last day to buy the stock and still receive the declared dividend

C) It marks the date when the stock price is adjusted for the dividend

D) It is the deadline for declaring dividends by the company

18. Market order guarantees:

A) Price

B) Execution

C) Timing

D) Quantity

19. A rights offering allows existing shareholders to:

A) Sell their shares back to the company at a predetermined price

B) Purchase additional shares at a discount before the public

C) Vote on important company decisions

D) Receive dividends before other shareholders

20. The book value of a stock is:

A) Based on the stock's market value

B) Calculated from the company's total tangible assets minus liabilities

C) The historical cost of the stock

D) Always higher than the market value

21. Penny stocks are characterized by:

A) High prices and low volatility

B) Low prices and potentially high volatility

C) Stable dividends

D) Large market capitalizations

22. Defensive stocks are:

A) Only found in the defense industry

B) Expected to provide consistent dividends and stability during market downturns

C) High-growth technology stocks

D) Associated with new market entrants

23. Which of the following best describes a "cyclical" stock?

A) A stock that performs well regardless of the economic cycle

B) A stock whose performance is closely tied to the economic cycle

C) A stock that offers consistent dividends

D) A stock from a company with a monopoly in its sector

24. What is the primary function of a stock exchange?

A) To provide loans to businesses

B) To facilitate the buying and selling of stocks

C) To regulate the national economy

D) To offer financial advice to investors

25. Which scenario would most likely lead to a stock's price increase?

A) An increase in the company's operational costs

B) A decrease in market interest rates

C) A scandal involving the company's CEO

D) A significant competitor entering the market

26. What does it mean when a stock is described as "overvalued"?

A) It is trading below its book value

B) It is trading at a price that exceeds its fundamental value

C) It has a low P/E ratio

D) It offers a high dividend yield

27. A "dividend reinvestment plan" (DRIP) allows investors to:

A) Receive all dividends in cash

B) Use dividends to purchase additional shares of the company's stock

C) Invest dividends in options

D) Transfer dividends to a tax-deferred account

28. Which type of order protects a stock's downside by triggering a sell at a certain price?

A) Limit order

B) Market order

C) Stop-loss order

D) Stop-limit order

29. What is the impact of a high turnover rate in a portfolio?

A) Increased tax efficiency

B) Decreased operational costs

C) Increased potential for higher returns

D) Increased transaction costs and potential tax implications

30. The term "sector rotation" refers to:

A) The cyclical process of dividends being reinvested

B) The movement of investments from one industry sector to another based on economic forecasts

C) The process of changing the CEO of a major corporation

D) The daily opening and closing of the stock market

31. An investor looking to hedge against a stock market downturn might invest in:

A) High beta stocks

B) Cyclical stocks

C) Treasury bonds

D) Technology stocks

32. The "bid" price of a stock refers to:

A) The highest price a seller is willing to accept

B) The price at which most shares are currently being sold

C) The lowest price a buyer is willing to pay

D) The last price at which the stock was traded

33. A company's "float" refers to:

A) The total number of shares available for trading by the public

B) The number of shares held by institutional investors

C) The total number of shares issued by the company

D) The number of shares available for short selling

34. Which statement about "penny stocks" is TRUE?

A) They are highly liquid

B) They are typically traded on major stock exchanges

C) They offer high dividends

D) They carry a high risk of loss

35. The "ask" price of a stock is:

A) The price a seller is willing to accept for the stock

B) Always lower than the bid price

C) The last price at which the stock was traded

D) Determined by the stock exchange

36. A "growth" investment strategy primarily focuses on:

A) Stocks that pay regular dividends

B) Stocks of companies expected to grow at an above-average rate compared to their industry

C) Bonds and other fixed-income securities

D) Real estate investments

37. What does the "ex-dividend" date signify for stock investors?

A) The date by which investors must hold the stock to receive the next dividend payment

B) The date on which dividends are paid out to shareholders

C) The deadline for declaring dividends for the next fiscal period

D) The date on which the stock price is adjusted to reflect the dividend payment

38. A mutual fund that specifically invests in companies with large market capitalizations is known as a:

A) Money market fund

B) Bond fund

C) Large-cap fund

D) Balanced fund

39. The "volume" of a stock traded refers to:

A) The total value of the stock traded during a specific period

B) The number of shares that were bought and sold during a specific period

C) The difference between the bid and ask prices

D) The number of shares available for trading

40. An "index fund" aims to:

A) Outperform the market

B) Replicate the performance of a specific market index

C) Focus exclusively on dividend-paying stocks

D) Invest in a single sector or industry

41. What is a "margin call"?

A) A request by a broker for the investor to deposit more money or securities into the account

B) A call to investors to sell their positions to avoid losses

C) An order to buy stocks at the lowest available price

D) A notification of dividends being paid

42. "Market depth" refers to:

A) The stability of the stock market

B) The extent to which a market can absorb large orders without impacting the price of a security

C) The number of stocks reaching their 52-week high

D) The overall economic impact of the stock market

43. A stock's "market order" is executed:

A) At a specified future date

B) At the best available price at the time of the order

C) Only if the stock reaches a certain price

D) Based on the trader's analysis and discretion

44. The "return on equity" (ROE) measures:

A) A company's debt levels

B) A company's efficiency at generating profits from every unit of shareholders' equity

C) The total dividends paid out to shareholders

D) The interest rate paid on the company's bonds

PACKAGED PRODUCTS

1. What is a mutual fund?

A) A single stock investment

B) A pool of funds collected from many investors for the purpose of investing in securities

C) A government-issued security

D) A type of insurance product

2. Which of the following is a characteristic of Exchange-Traded Funds (ETFs)?

A) They can only be bought at the end of the trading day

B) They offer the diversification of a mutual fund but trade like a stock

C) They guarantee fixed returns

D) They are not subject to market fluctuations

3. What is the primary advantage of investing in a mutual fund?

A) Guaranteed returns

B) Professional management

C) Fixed interest rates

D) Exemption from taxes

4. Which type of investment vehicle is most likely to track an index?

A) Hedge fund

B) ETF

C) Money market fund

D) Certificate of Deposit (CD)

5. A real estate investment trust (REIT) primarily invests in:

A) Stocks and bonds

B) Real estate and real estate-related assets

C) Commodities like gold and silver

D) Cryptocurrencies

6. What distinguishes a closed-end fund from an open-end fund?

A) Closed-end funds are not traded on stock exchanges

B) Closed-end funds have a fixed number of shares and are traded like stocks

C) Open-end funds can be bought and sold throughout the trading day

D) Open-end funds do not charge management fees

7. Which of the following best describes a hedge fund?

A) A fund that primarily invests in government securities

B) A private investment partnership open to a limited number of investors and requires a significant initial minimum investment

C) A fund that offers shares to the general public with no minimum investment

D) A fund that guarantees returns by hedging all investments

8. Unit Investment Trusts (UITs) differ from mutual funds in that UITs:

A) Have a professionally managed portfolio that changes frequently

B) Offer a fixed portfolio of securities with a definite termination date

C) Allow investors to vote on investment choices

D) Operate without a board of directors or investment advisor

9. Which of the following is true about money market funds?

A) They invest primarily in high-risk securities

B) They aim to maintain a stable share price and offer liquidity

C) They offer high returns with high volatility

D) They are insured by the Federal Deposit Insurance Corporation (FDIC)

10. An investor seeking tax-exempt income might consider investing in:

A) Corporate bonds

B) Municipal bond funds

C) International funds

D) Commodity funds

11. Target-date funds are primarily designed for investors who:

A) Seek aggressive growth without regard to time

B) Are interested in a fixed return rate

C) Are saving for a specific goal with a known time horizon, like retirement

D) Prefer to actively manage their investment choices

12. The expense ratio of a mutual fund or ETF refers to:

A) The ratio of the fund's transactions to its assets

B) The total return of the fund over a year

C) The annual fee that all funds charge their shareholders

D) The fund's ability to outperform the market

13. Which of the following investments is considered the most liquid?

A) Real estate

B) ETFs

C) Private equity

D) Collectibles

14. Sector funds invest in:

A) Government and corporate bonds exclusively

B) A specific sector of the economy, such as technology or healthcare

C) A diversified portfolio across all sectors

D) International markets only

15. The net asset value (NAV) of a mutual fund is:

A) The total value of the fund's holdings minus its liabilities, divided by the number of shares outstanding

B) A fixed value that does not change

C) Determined by the stock market

D) The price at which the fund borrows money

16. Balanced funds aim to:

A) Invest 100% in stocks for growth

B) Provide a mix of growth, income, and stability through a portfolio of stocks, bonds, and other securities

C) Focus exclusively on high-yield bonds

D) Invest solely in international markets

17. An advantage of investing in an index fund is:

A) Active management to outperform the market

B) High potential for above-market returns

C) Lower expense ratios compared to actively managed funds

D) Guaranteed returns

18. A fund that pools money from many investors to buy a portfolio of precious metals is known as a:

A) Commodity fund

B) Balanced fund

C) Bond fund

D) Money market fund

19. Which statement about ETFs is NOT true?

A) ETFs offer the advantage of intraday trading

B) ETFs typically have lower expense ratios than mutual funds

C) All ETFs track an index

D) ETFs can be bought and sold like individual stocks

20. International funds invest in:

A) Only domestic stocks and bonds

B) Securities from markets outside the investor's country of residence

C) Real estate exclusively

D) Commodities traded internationally

21. The primary risk of investing in a sector fund is:

A) Currency risk

B) Credit risk

C) Market risk

D) Lack of diversification

22. Dividend income funds focus on investing in:

A) Companies that do not pay dividends

B) Companies with a high potential for capital appreciation

C) Companies that pay regular, high dividends

D) Fixed-income securities only

23. An investor seeking to minimize risk while ensuring capital preservation might choose which of the following?

A) Commodity funds

B) Money market funds

C) Sector funds

D) International funds

24. Which of the following is a feature unique to ETFs compared to mutual funds?

A) Professional management

B) Diversification

C) Intraday trading

D) Annual fees

25. A balanced fund is designed to:

A) Invest solely in bonds to ensure fixed income

B) Allocate investments across various asset classes to balance risk and return

C) Focus on high-growth stocks with no dividend payout

D) Invest in commodities like gold and oil

26. What is the primary goal of an income fund?

A) Capital appreciation

B) Regular income generation through dividends or interest payments

C) Long-term growth through reinvestment of earnings

D) Speculative trading for quick profits

27. Which type of fund primarily aims at capital protection and provides returns through dividends from utility companies?

A) Growth fund

B) Utility fund

C) Index fund

D) Hedge fund

28. The risk of investing in an international fund includes:

A) Currency risk

B) Lower volatility

C) Guaranteed returns

D) Domestic economic stability

29. What distinguishes a no-load fund from a load fund?

A) No management fees

B) No buying or selling fees

C) A fixed number of shares

D) Trades on stock exchanges

30. Which investment vehicle is known for pooling money to invest in a portfolio of short-term, high-quality debt securities?

A) Bond funds

B) Money market funds

C) Equity funds

D) Hedge funds

31. An index fund that tracks the S&P 500 is designed to:

A) Outperform the S&P 500

B) Mirror the performance of the S&P 500

C) Focus solely on the top 10 companies in the S&P 500

D) Invest in companies outside the S&P 500 for diversification

32. A fund that uses strategies like leverage, short-selling, and derivatives to amplify returns is most likely a:

A) Mutual fund

B) Hedge fund

C) Money market fund

D) Balanced fund

33. The term "actively managed fund" refers to a fund:

A) That changes its investment strategy daily

B) Where the fund manager makes decisions about how to invest the fund's money

C) That only invests in active market hours

D) Without a fixed strategy, investing randomly

34. Which of the following best describes a "fund of funds"?

A) A fund that invests directly in stocks and bonds

B) A fund that invests in other mutual funds or ETFs

C) A fund with a fixed investment objective

D) A fund that only invests in government securities

35. The advantage of a target-date fund is its:

A) High-risk, high-return investment strategy

B) Automatic adjustment of asset allocation as the target date approaches

C) Single-sector investment focus for specialization

D) Fixed dividend payout rate

36. Which of the following investments typically offers tax advantages?

A) Corporate bond funds

B) Municipal bond funds

C) International funds

D) Sector funds

37. An ETF that seeks to return the inverse of the performance of its benchmark index is called a(n):

A) Index ETF

B) Leveraged ETF

C) Inverse ETF

D) Balanced ETF

38. A characteristic of high yield bond funds is:

A) Low risk and low return

B) Investment in bonds rated below investment grade

C) Focus on government securities

D) Stability in market downturns

39. The primary reason investors choose socially responsible funds is to:

A) Ensure high returns regardless of the market condition

B) Invest in companies that align with their ethical, social, and environmental values

C) Avoid taxes on investment returns

D) Gain exposure to high-risk markets

40. Which type of investment is designed to provide a hedge against inflation?

A) Fixed-income funds

B) Real estate investment trusts (REITs)

C) Money market funds

D) Corporate bond funds

41. Asset allocation funds differ from other mutual funds in that they:

A) Invest only in stocks

B) Automatically adjust their portfolio based on market conditions

C) Maintain a fixed allocation of assets among stocks, bonds, and cash

D) Focus exclusively on international investments

42. A characteristic feature of a "leveraged ETF" is that it:

A) Aims to deliver multiples of the daily performance of the index it tracks

B) Guarantees a fixed return

C) Offers a diversified investment in a single sector

D) Tracks the performance of the bond market

43. Venture capital funds are unique because they:

A) Invest in mature, dividend-paying companies

B) Provide capital to start-up companies with high growth potential

C) Focus on investing in government securities

D) Offer fixed monthly returns to investors

44. The primary benefit of investing in a global fund over an international fund is:

A) Exposure to a single country's market

B) Investment in both U.S. and non-U.S. markets

C) Focus on emerging markets only

D) Avoiding currency risk

OPTIONS

1. What is the primary purpose of buying a call option?

A) To sell a stock at a predetermined price

B) To buy a stock at a predetermined price

C) To hedge against a decline in stock price

D) To earn dividends from stock ownership

2. An investor sells a put option. What does this indicate about their market expectation?

A) They expect the market to rise

B) They expect the market to fall

C) They are looking for dividend income

D) They want to buy the underlying stock at a higher price

3. Which of the following best describes a covered call strategy?

A) Selling a call option without owning the underlying stock

B) Buying a call option to cover a short position in the stock

C) Selling a call option while owning the equivalent amount of the underlying stock

D) Buying a call option to hedge against a decline in stock price

4. What is the strike price of an option?

A) The price at which an option can be exercised

B) The market price of the stock when the option is sold

C) The difference between the market price and the exercise price

D) The price paid for the option premium

5. Which option position benefits from an increase in volatility?

A) Short call

B) Long put

C) Long straddle

D) Short straddle

6. What does it mean to be 'in the money' for a call option?

A) The strike price is above the market price of the underlying asset

B) The strike price is below the market price of the underlying asset

C) The option cannot be exercised profitably

D) The option's premium is at its lowest point

7. What is the maximum loss for a buyer of a put option?

A) Unlimited

B) The premium paid for the option

C) The strike price of the option

D) The difference between the strike price and the stock price

8. An investor writes a naked put. What risk are they exposed to?

A) The stock's price increasing above the strike price

B) The stock's price falling below the strike price

C) Paying dividends on the underlying stock

D) The option expiring worthless

9. Which of the following is true about American-style options?

A) They can only be exercised at expiration

B) They can be exercised at any time before expiration

C) They are typically less expensive than European-style options

D) They can only be bought and sold in the European market

10. What is an option's premium?

A) The maximum profit an option can achieve

B) The cost to buy the option contract

C) The difference between the strike price and the stock price

D) The dividend paid by the underlying stock

11. The breakeven point for a call option buyer is:

A) The strike price plus the premium paid

B) The strike price minus the premium paid

C) The current stock price plus the premium paid

D) The current stock price minus the premium paid

12. What strategy involves buying both a call and a put option on the same stock with the same expiration and strike price?

A) Covered call

B) Straddle

C) Spread

D) Collar

13. The intrinsic value of a put option increases as:

A) The underlying stock's price increases

B) The underlying stock's price decreases

C) The expiration date approaches

D) The volatility decreases

14. What does the term 'expiration date' in options trading refer to?

A) The last date on which the option can be exercised

B) The date when the option was issued

C) The date by which the option must be sold

D) The date on which the option's premium is paid

15. A protective put strategy is used to:

A) Generate income from stock ownership

B) Speculate on a stock's decline

C) Protect against a decline in the value of owned stock

D) Increase leverage on a stock investment

16. What is the outcome if an option expires 'out of the money'?

A) The option can still be exercised at a loss

B) The option's premium is refunded

C) The option expires worthless

D) The option is automatically exercised

17. The delta of an option measures:

A) The option's sensitivity to changes in the volatility of the underlying asset

B) The option's time decay

C) The change in the option's price for a one-point move in the underlying asset

D) The option's premium as a percentage of the stock price

18. Which of the following options positions is considered the most risky?

A) Buying a call

B) Selling a naked call

C) Buying a put

D) Selling a covered call

19. The 'time value' of an option refers to:

A) The option's premium above its intrinsic value

B) The difference between the strike price and the stock price

C) The amount the option is 'in the money'

D) The fixed time until the option's expiration

20. A call option is said to be 'at the money' when:

A) The strike price is significantly above the stock price

B) The strike price is significantly below the stock price

C) The strike price is equal to the current market price of the underlying stock

D) The option's time value is zero

21. Which strategy might an investor use if they expect a stock's price to move significantly but are unsure of the direction?

A) Bull spread

B) Bear spread

C) Long straddle

D) Short straddle

22. The implied volatility of an option indicates:

A) The historical volatility of the stock

B) The expected volatility of the stock price until expiration

C) The difference between the strike price and the stock price

D) The time value of the option

23. Which of the following outcomes is possible when an investor sells a covered call option?

A) Unlimited loss potential

B) The stock is called away if the stock price exceeds the strike price

C) The option can only be exercised at expiration

D) The seller receives the stock if the option is exercised

24. What does the 'theta' of an option represent?

A) The rate of change of the option's price with respect to the underlying stock's price

B) The option's sensitivity to changes in volatility

C) The rate at which the option's price decays over time

D) The change in the option's delta for a one-point move in the underlying asset

25. A put option is considered 'deep in the money' when:

A) The strike price is slightly below the current market price of the stock

B) The strike price is significantly higher than the current market price of the stock

C) The option's time value is zero

D) The option's intrinsic value is less than its premium

26. Which strategy involves selling a put option and buying a call option with the same expiration date and strike price?

A) Bull spread

B) Bear spread

C) Synthetic long stock

D) Protective put

27. The primary benefit of using options in a portfolio is:

A) To increase the portfolio's exposure to dividends

B) To hedge against potential losses

C) To eliminate the risk of loss

D) To guarantee a fixed rate of return

28. An investor buys a call option and sells a put option with the same strike price and expiration. This strategy is known as a:

A) Straddle

B) Strangle

C) Synthetic long stock

D) Collar

29. The gamma of an option measures:

A) The rate of change of the option's delta

B) The option's time decay

C) The option's sensitivity to interest rate changes

D) The option's premium in relation to the strike price

30. Which of the following best describes the risk profile of selling a naked call option?

A) Limited profit potential and unlimited loss potential

B) Unlimited profit potential and limited loss potential

C) Limited profit potential and limited loss potential

D) Unlimited profit potential and unlimited loss potential

31. The vega of an option indicates how the option's price changes with:

A) A change in the risk-free interest rate

B) A 1% change in the implied volatility of the underlying asset

C) A change in the dividend yield of the underlying asset

D) The passage of time

32. A collar strategy in options trading involves:

A) Buying a call and a put with the same strike price and expiration

B) Selling a call and buying a put with different strike prices but the same expiration

C) Buying a call and selling a put with the same strike price and expiration

D) Owning the underlying stock, buying a put, and selling a call to hedge against downside risk

33. Which of the following is a characteristic of an 'at the money' put option?

A) The strike price is significantly below the current market price of the stock

B) The strike price is significantly above the current market price of the stock

C) The strike price is equal to the current market price of the underlying stock

D) The option cannot be exercised profitably

34. The intrinsic value of a call option is calculated as:

A) The current stock price minus the strike price, if positive; otherwise, zero

B) The strike price minus the current stock price, if positive; otherwise, zero

C) The premium paid for the option minus the current stock price

D) The strike price plus the premium paid for the option

35. An investor looking to profit from a decrease in a stock's price without owning the stock might use:

A) A long call strategy

B) A long put strategy

C) A covered call strategy

D) A synthetic long stock strategy

36. The maximum profit for a long put option holder is:

A) Limited to the premium paid for the option

B) The strike price minus the premium paid, if the stock goes to zero

C) Unlimited as the stock price falls

D) The premium received for selling the option

37. Which option strategy is best suited for an investor expecting a moderate increase in the underlying stock's price?

A) Buying a put

B) Selling a naked call

C) Buying a call

D) Selling a put

38. The break-even point for a put option seller is:

A) The strike price plus the premium received

B) The strike price minus the premium received

C) The current stock price plus the premium received

D) The current stock price minus the premium received

39. An option with no intrinsic value and only time value is said to be:

A) In the money

B) At the money

C) Out of the money

D) Deep in the money

40. A risk reversal strategy in options trading involves:

A) Buying a call and selling a put with the same expiration and strike price

B) Selling a call and buying a put with the same expiration and strike price

C) Buying a call and a put with the same expiration but different strike prices

D) Selling a call and a put with the same expiration but different strike prices

41. The primary reason for an investor to use a bear spread is to:

A) Profit from a bullish market

B) Limit loss potential in a bearish market

C) Capitalize on market volatility

D) Hedge against a decline in the underlying asset's price

42. Which of the following describes the leverage effect of options?

A) The ability to control a large amount of the underlying asset with a relatively small investment

B) The reduction of risk through diversification

C) The guarantee of a fixed return on the option

D) The elimination of time decay

43. The 'rho' of an option measures:

A) The sensitivity of the option's price to changes in the underlying stock's dividend yield

B) The sensitivity of the option's price to changes in interest rates

C) The change in the option's price for a one-point move in the underlying asset

D) The rate at which the option's price decays over time

44. A butterfly spread involves:

A) Buying one call option and selling two call options at a higher strike price

B) Buying two call options at different strike prices and selling one call option at a middle strike price

C) Selling a call and a put option at the same strike price and buying a call and put option at higher and lower strike prices, respectively

D) Buying a call and put option at the same strike price and selling a call and put option at higher and lower strike prices, respectively

Understanding Trading, Customer Accounts, and Prohibited Activities

TYPES OF ORDERS

1. What is the primary purpose of a market order?

A) To guarantee a specific price

B) To execute a trade immediately at the best available price

C) To limit loss

D) To buy or sell at a price that is not currently available

2. A limit order is used when:

A) Speed of execution is more important than price

B) A trader wants to specify the maximum or minimum price at which they are willing to buy or sell

C) An investor wishes to trade a stock at its current market price

D) Protecting against market volatility is not a concern

3. What does a stop-loss order do?

A) Guarantees a profit on a stock

B) Buys a stock when it reaches a certain price

C) Sells a stock when it falls to a certain price to limit an investor's loss

D) Prevents a stock from being sold at a loss

4. Which order becomes a market order once the stop price is reached?

A) Limit order

B) Stop order

C) Stop-limit order

D) Market order

5. A stop-limit order:

A) Executes at a specified price or better after a given stop price has been reached

B) Immediately sells a stock when it hits a certain price

C) Converts into a market order at the stop price

D) Has no specified limit on the execution price

6. Which type of order can help protect profits on a stock that an investor owns?

A) Market order

B) Limit order

C) Stop-loss order

D) Stop-limit order

7. What is the main difference between a stop order and a stop-limit order?

A) A stop order specifies a price, while a stop-limit order does not

B) A stop-limit order specifies a price, while a stop order becomes a market order

C) A stop order is for buying only, while a stop-limit order is for selling only

D) There is no difference; they are the same

8. An investor places a limit order to sell a stock at $50. What happens if the stock's price jumps to $55?

A) The order is not executed because the price is too high

B) The order may be executed at $55

C) The order is canceled automatically

D) The order is executed at exactly $50

9. Which order type might an investor use to enter a position at a specific price or better?

A) Market order

B) Limit order

C) Stop order

D) Stop-limit order

10. If an investor wants to sell a stock as it falls to limit losses, which order type should they use?

A) Limit sell order

B) Market sell order

C) Stop-loss order

D) Stop-limit sell order

11. What is the risk of placing a stop-loss order on a stock?

A) The stock may rebound after the order is executed

B) The order may not be executed if the stock price rises

C) The order guarantees a specific execution price

D) There is no risk associated with stop-loss orders

12. A GTC (Good Till Canceled) order:

A) Must be executed by the end of the trading day

B) Remains active until it is executed or canceled by the trader

C) Is automatically canceled if not executed within 24 hours

D) Can only be placed during regular market hours

13. Which order type is likely to result in the highest execution price for a sell order when the market is rapidly rising?

A) Limit order

B) Market order

C) Stop order

D) Stop-limit order

14. An all-or-none (AON) order is:

A) An order to buy or sell a stock that must be executed in its entirety or not at all

B) A type of market order that is executed immediately

C) An order that allows partial fills

D) Only used for buying securities, not selling

15. The primary advantage of using a limit order over a market order is:

A) Speed of execution

B) The ability to specify a price

C) The guarantee of execution

D) Flexibility in order size

16. In volatile markets, a stop-limit order:

A) Provides a guarantee that the order will be executed at the stop price

B) May not execute if the stock price moves past the limit price too quickly

C) Converts to a market order for immediate execution

D) Eliminates the risk of slippage

17. What happens if the limit price of a stop-limit order is not reached?

A) The order is executed at the next best available price

B) The order remains active until the limit price is reached or the order is canceled

C) The order is automatically converted to a market order

D) The order is executed at the stop price

18. A day order:

A) Is valid for 60 days from the date it is placed

B) Expires if not executed by the close of the trading day it was placed

C) Can be executed at any time regardless of market conditions

D) Is only executed at the day's highest price

19. Which scenario best uses a limit order to buy?

A) An investor wants to purchase a stock at its current market price

B) An investor wants to purchase a stock only if it drops to a certain price or lower

C) An investor is looking to sell a stock at a specific price

D) An investor wants to ensure the stock is bought immediately

20. The execution of a stop order depends on:

A) The stock reaching a specific price

B) The time of day

C) The volume of trades for the stock

D) The difference between the bid and ask prices

21. Fill or kill (FOK) orders require that:

A) The order be executed immediately in its entirety or not at all

B) The order be partially filled

C) The order remains active until the end of the trading day

D) The order be executed over several days

22. Which of the following is true about market orders?

A) They are always executed at the bid price for buys and the ask price for sells

B) They offer the best protection against price volatility

C) They ensure execution but not a specific price

D) They are used to guarantee price rather than execution

23. What is the primary advantage of a trailing stop order?

A) It locks in profits while potentially allowing for further gains

B) It guarantees execution at a specific price

C) It remains active for multiple trading sessions

D) It allows for buying and selling at the same time

24. A discretionary order:

A) Must be executed immediately

B) Allows the broker to decide the best time and price to execute the order

C) Is always a limit order

D) Is illegal in most markets

25. What happens when a limit order to buy is placed above the current market price?

A) The order is executed immediately

B) The order is likely to be executed as the price falls

C) The order is canceled automatically

D) The order is converted to a market order

26. In a fast-moving market, what is the risk associated with a market order?

A) The order may be executed at a very different price from the current price (slippage)

B) The order will not be executed

C) The order will be executed at the lowest possible price

D) The order will be delayed until the market stabilizes

27. A buy stop order is typically used to:

A) Limit a loss on a short sale

B) Prevent buying a stock at too high a price

C) Lock in profits on a long position

D) Buy a stock after it falls to a certain price

28. Which of the following best describes a bracket order?

A) An order that allows buying and selling at the same time

B) An order that sets a stop loss and take profit level at the same time

C) An order that must be executed in parts over several days

D) An order that is valid only during a specific trading session

29. A market-if-touched (MIT) order is:

A) An order to buy (or sell) a stock at a specified price or better

B) Similar to a limit order, but executed only if the market price touches the order price

C) An order that becomes active only if a certain price level is reached

D) A type of stop order that is executed at the best available price after being triggered

30. The primary use of a stop order in a long position is to:

A) Ensure the purchase of additional shares at a lower price

B) Protect against a significant drop in the stock's price

C) Guarantee a profit on the investment

D) Buy more shares as the stock's price increases

31. A sell stop-limit order:

A) Is executed at the stop price once it is reached

B) Becomes a limit order to sell when the stock falls to the stop price

C) Guarantees the sale of the stock at the stop price

D) Is used to buy stock at a lower price

32. What is a 'not held' order?

A) An order that gives the broker discretion over the execution timing and price

B) An order that cannot be executed due to market conditions

C) An order that is suspended until a specific event occurs

D) An order that remains inactive until the client confirms it

33. A market-on-close (MOC) order is:

A) Executed immediately at the current market price

B) An order to buy or sell a stock at the closing price of the market

C) A limit order that is only active in the last hour of trading

D) A stop order that activates at market close

34. The main purpose of an iceberg order is to:

A) Hide the true size of an order by revealing only a small portion of it at a time

B) Freeze the price of a stock for a certain period

C) Ensure the execution of a large order at a single price

D) Allow for simultaneous buying and selling of a stock

35. A pegged order is one that:

A) Is fixed at a set price and does not change

B) Is adjusted based on changes in a benchmark rate or index

C) Must be executed at the opening price of the market

D) Is linked to the performance of a related security

36. In which scenario would a day trader most likely use a market order?

A) When seeking to buy a stock at a very specific price

B) To quickly enter or exit a position to capitalize on market movements

C) To set a maximum price for buying a stock

D) To hold a position overnight

37. A limit order book is used by traders to:

A) View all active limit orders for a particular stock

B) Record profits and losses for the day

C) Keep track of market orders only

D) Monitor the performance of their investment portfolio

38. What is the primary risk of using a good-till-canceled (GTC) order?

A) The order may be forgotten and executed at an undesirable time

B) The order cannot be canceled once placed

C) The order is only valid for very short-term trades

D) The order does not allow for price adjustments

39. A fill-or-kill (FOK) order is most appropriate when:

A) An investor wants to ensure a position is closed by the end of the day

B) The investor requires immediate and complete execution of a large order

C) The investor is looking to buy a stock and hold it long-term

D) The stock being traded has low liquidity

40. A time-in-force condition on an order determines:

A) The price at which the order should be executed

B) The duration for which the order is active

C) The exact time the order should be executed

D) The number of shares to be traded in the order

41. What is the main advantage of using a volume-weighted average price (VWAP) order?

A) It guarantees the order will be executed at the day's highest price

B) It helps in buying or selling a stock at a price close to the average price of the day

C) It ensures execution at a fixed price

D) It allows trading at multiple prices in one day

42. The execution of a hidden (or iceberg) order:

A) Is visible to all market participants

B) Shows only a part of the order size to the market to avoid large price movements

C) Cannot be modified once placed

D) Is executed at the end of the trading day regardless of price

43. A sweep-to-fill order is designed to:

A) Execute at a single price point

B) Be filled at the opening price of the stock

C) Sweep through multiple price levels to fill the order as quickly as possible

D) Fill only at the closing price of the trading session

44. The use of a conditional order allows an investor to:

A) Set conditions under which the order will automatically be executed or canceled

B) Trade without any limitations on price or time

C) Execute trades based on the performance of a related security

D) Avoid all risks associated with market volatility

ACCOUNT TYPES
----

1. What distinguishes a cash account from a margin account?

A) The ability to borrow funds from the broker

B) The requirement to pay for securities in full at the time of purchase

C) The types of securities that can be purchased

D) The ability to participate in options trading

2. Which account type allows an investor to short sell securities?

A) Cash account

B) Margin account

C) Retirement account

D) Trust account

3. What is a primary advantage of using a Roth IRA over a traditional IRA?

A) Contributions are tax-deductible

B) Withdrawals in retirement are tax-free

C) No early withdrawal penalties

D) No annual contribution limits

4. A joint tenancy with right of survivorship (JTWROS) account automatically:

A) Divides assets equally among all account holders

B) Transfers ownership of the account to the surviving account holders upon one's death

C) Requires all account holders to approve transactions

D) Limits withdrawals to a certain percentage per account holder

5. What is the main feature of a Uniform Gifts to Minors Act (UGMA) account?

A) It allows minors to trade stocks without adult supervision

B) It is managed by a custodian until the minor reaches a certain age

C) It offers tax advantages for the custodian

D) It restricts the types of investments that can be made

6. Which type of account is specifically designed for saving for education expenses?

A) 529 Plan

B) Roth IRA

C) Health Savings Account (HSA)

D) Coverdell Education Savings Account (ESA)

7. What is the primary function of a trust account?

A) To allow trading on margin

B) To manage assets for the benefit of a third party

C) To consolidate business transactions

D) To provide tax-free investment income

8. In which type of account does the broker have the authority to make trades without the client's specific approval for each trade?

A) Discretionary account

B) Cash account

C) Margin account

D) Managed account

9. A Transfer on Death (TOD) designation in an account:

A) Allows for the transfer of assets to a designated beneficiary upon the account holder's death

B) Requires the account to be settled in probate court

C) Is only available for retirement accounts

D) Transfers the account to a trust upon the account holder's death

10. What is the main characteristic of a corporate investment account?

A) It is used for individual retirement planning

B) It allows employees to buy stock in their company

C) It is opened in the name of a corporation for investment purposes

D) It provides personal liability protection for individual investors

11. An individual retirement account (IRA) offers which of the following benefits?

A) The ability to trade on margin

B) Tax advantages on either contributions or withdrawals

C) Unlimited contributions

D) The ability to take loans against the account

12. What is a prime brokerage account?

A) An account for beginner investors with limited services

B) A service offered to large investors and institutions that consolidates various services

C) A type of account that offers the lowest commission rates

D) An account that only offers trading in prime rate securities

13. A custodial account under the Uniform Transfers to Minors Act (UTMA) differs from a UGMA account by:

A) Allowing for a wider range of assets to be gifted

B) Restricting the use of funds to educational expenses

C) Offering tax benefits to the custodian

D) Limiting contributions to cash only

14. The main advantage of a tax-deferred retirement account is:

A) Immediate tax benefits on contributions

B) The ability to withdraw funds at any time without penalty

C) Tax-free growth of investments until withdrawal

D) No required minimum distributions

15. A Coverdell ESA is unique because:

A) It allows for tax-free withdrawals for qualified education expenses

B) It can only be used for post-secondary education expenses

C) Contributions are tax-deductible

D) There are no contribution limits

16. Which account type is best suited for an investor looking to trade securities internationally?

A) Domestic brokerage account

B) Forex account

C) Global trading account

D) Margin account

17. A Health Savings Account (HSA) is designed to:

A) Provide a way to save for retirement on a tax-deferred basis

B) Offer tax advantages for saving and paying for healthcare expenses

C) Invest in healthcare-related stocks and bonds

D) Cover educational expenses related to health and medicine

18. An accredited investor account is for individuals who:

A) Have passed a specific financial accreditation test

B) Meet certain income or net worth criteria, allowing access to higher-risk investments

C) Are certified financial planners or investment advisors

D) Hold a degree in finance or a related field

19. The primary benefit of a sweep account is to:

A) Allow investors to write checks against their investment account

B) Automatically invest excess cash balances for short-term gains

C) Provide overdraft protection

D) Sweep profits into tax-advantaged accounts

20. A Solo 401(k) plan is ideal for:

A) Employees of large corporations

B) Self-employed individuals with no employees other than a spouse

C) Investors looking for a hands-off retirement plan

D) Anyone without access to an employer-sponsored retirement plan

21. A money purchase pension plan requires:

A) Employers to make fixed, annual contributions to employees' retirement accounts

B) Employees to contribute a fixed percentage of their salary annually

C) Both employers and employees to make matching contributions

D) Voluntary contributions from employees only

22. What is the primary feature of a limited trading authorization in a brokerage account?

A) It allows the account holder to limit the types of securities that can be traded

B) It grants a designated individual the ability to make trades on behalf of the account holder, within certain limits

C) It restricts trading to a specified number of transactions per month

D) It limits the account to trading only during specific market hours

23. Which account type is specifically designed for high-net-worth individuals offering personalized investment strategies and services?

A) Discount brokerage account

B) Managed account

C) Trust account

D) Custodial account

24. A brokerage firm offers an account that automatically moves cash balances into a higher interest-earning money market fund at the end of each day. This account is known as:

A) A sweep account

B) A margin account

C) A cash management account

D) An interest-bearing account

25. Which type of account would be most suitable for an investor looking to execute large volume trades with minimal impact on the market price?

A) Standard brokerage account

B) Prime brokerage account

C) Dark pool account

D) Omnibus account

26. An investor interested in a tax-efficient way to gift large sums of money to their children might use:

A) A joint account

B) A custodial account

C) A discretionary account

D) A trust account

27. For an investor primarily interested in investing in mutual funds, which account type might offer the most benefits?

A) A mutual fund wrap account

B) A forex trading account

C) A direct stock purchase plan

D) A standard brokerage account

28. An account that consolidates banking and brokerage services, offering features like check writing and debit cards, is known as:

A) A cash account

B) A cash management account

C) A margin account

D) A direct access trading account

29. Which account type allows investors to pool their resources to meet minimum investment requirements of certain funds or securities?

A) Club account

B) Joint tenancy account

C) Investment club account

D) Partnership account

30. An account set up specifically for the purpose of holding and managing securities for an investor by a financial institution, which acts as the legal owner on behalf of the investor, is called:

A) A nominee account

B) A discretionary account

C) A managed account

D) A custodial account

31. What type of account is designed for investors who wish to borrow against the value of their securities for purposes other than purchasing more securities?

A) A loan account

B) A margin loan account

C) A securities-based loan account

D) A collateral account

32. An account that offers investors the ability to invest in a diversified portfolio of stocks and bonds as a single investment is known as:

A) An ETF managed account

B) A mutual fund

C) A target-date fund account

D) A balanced fund account

33. Which account type is best suited for an investor who wants to trade securities anonymously?

A) An anonymous trading account

B) A dark pool account

C) A numbered account

D) A private trading account

34. An account that is managed without the investor's day-to-day involvement, where investment decisions are made by a designated financial advisor or portfolio manager, is called:

A) A self-directed account

B) An automated trading account

C) A discretionary managed account

D) A robo-advisor account

35. For an investor looking to save for healthcare expenses with pre-tax dollars, which account type would be most appropriate?

A) Flexible Spending Account (FSA)

B) Health Savings Account (HSA)

C) Medical Savings Account (MSA)

D) Health Reimbursement Account (HRA)

36. An account that allows for the trading of futures contracts and options on futures is known as:

A) A futures account

B) A commodities trading account

C) A derivatives trading account

D) A speculative account

37. An investor who wants to participate in the initial public offering (IPO) market would most likely need to have:

A) A standard brokerage account

B) An IPO account

C) A prime brokerage account

D) An accredited investor account

38. A type of account that is designed for saving for retirement with after-tax contributions and tax-free growth is:

A) A 401(k) plan

B) A Roth IRA

C) A traditional IRA

D) A SEP IRA

39. An account that allows employees to purchase company stock at a discount as part of their employee benefits is known as:

A) An employee stock purchase plan (ESPP)

B) A direct stock purchase plan (DSPP)

C) A stock option plan

D) A restricted stock unit (RSU) account

40. Which account type is specifically designed for saving for retirement and allows for pre-tax contributions by the employer on behalf of the employee?

A) A profit-sharing plan

B) A defined benefit plan

C) A defined contribution plan

D) A SIMPLE IRA

41. An account that allows investors to automatically reinvest dividends from stocks or mutual funds into additional shares is known as:

A) A dividend reinvestment plan (DRIP)

B) A compound interest account

C) A growth account

D) A capital gains account

42. For an investor looking to execute trades based on algorithmic trading strategies, which account type would be most suitable?

A) An algorithmic trading account

B) A high-frequency trading (HFT) account

C) A quantitative analysis account

D) A direct market access (DMA) account

43. An account designed for the purpose of saving for post-secondary education expenses that offers tax advantages is:

A) A Coverdell Education Savings Account (ESA)

B) A 529 college savings plan

C) A custodial account

D) A scholarship fund account

44. Which account type offers investors the opportunity to lend their securities to others, often for the purpose of short selling, in exchange for a lending fee?

A) A securities lending account

B) A margin account

C) A short selling account

D) A brokerage lending account

PROHIBITED PRACTICES

1. What is considered a prohibited practice in the securities industry?

A) Diversification

B) Churning

C) Dollar-cost averaging

D) Rebalancing

2. Churning refers to:

A) The process of switching clients between mutual funds to achieve diversification.

B) Excessive trading in a client's account to generate commissions.

C) Investing in volatile stocks to maximize returns.

D) Regularly rebalancing a portfolio to maintain a desired asset allocation.

3. Front-running is the unethical practice of:

A) Executing orders on behalf of the firm before client orders.

B) Placing trades based on insider information.

C) Delaying client orders to benefit from price changes.

D) Trading securities before the market opens.

4. Which of the following is considered a manipulative trading practice?

A) Buy and hold strategy

B) Market making

C) Pump and dump

D) Value investing

5. Painting the tape involves:

A) Creating a misleading appearance of active trading in a security to attract investors.

B) Using a dark pool to execute large trades without impacting the market.

C) Decorating the trading floor with colorful tape to indicate market trends.

D) Marking the close by executing trades at the end of the trading day to influence the closing price.

6. The use of non-public, material information to make investment decisions is known as:

A) Arbitrage

B) Insider trading

C) Hedging

D) Speculation

7. A wash sale occurs when:

A) A security is sold at a loss, and a substantially identical security is purchased within 30 days before or after the sale.

B) Securities are washed through multiple accounts to hide the true owner.

C) A trader cleans up their portfolio by selling non-performing assets.

D) Securities are sold through a car wash fundraiser.

8. Marking the close refers to:

A) The practice of placing trades at the end of the trading day to affect the closing price of a stock.

B) Closing all open positions at the end of the trading day.

C) The process of updating the market close prices on the exchange's website.

D) Celebrating the end of the trading day with a ceremonial bell ringing.

9. The illegal practice of selling a security without owning it or ensuring its availability for delivery is known as:

A) Naked short selling

B) Covered short selling

C) Margin trading

D) Leveraged buying

10. Spoofing in the context of trading refers to:

A) Wearing disguises on the trading floor to confuse competitors.

B) The practice of submitting large orders to create the illusion of interest in a stock, then canceling them.

C) Creating fake news to influence stock prices.

D) Impersonating another trader to execute unauthorized trades.

11. Layering, a form of market manipulation, involves:

A) Placing and then canceling orders to mislead other traders about the demand or supply of a security.

B) Stacking trades in a particular order to benefit from price movements.

C) Using multiple layers of security to protect trade information.

D) Investing in securities across different layers of the capital structure.

12. The act of using misleading or false statements to sell investments is known as:

A) Arbitrage

B) Misrepresentation

C) Diversification

D) Asset allocation

13. Unauthorized trading occurs when:

A) A broker executes trades in a client's account without the client's specific approval.

B) A client trades without informing their broker.

C) Trading is done outside of authorized trading hours.

D) Trades are executed in an unauthorized security.

14. The practice of recommending securities without a reasonable basis for the recommendation is known as:

A) Suitability violation

B) Fundamental analysis

C) Technical analysis

D) Quantitative analysis

15. Failing to disclose conflicts of interest to clients is considered:

A) A best practice in certain jurisdictions.

B) Ethical in cases where the conflict is minimal.

C) A violation of ethical standards.

D) Acceptable if the client does not inquire.

16. The act of guaranteeing a client that they will not lose money on a particular securities transaction is known as:

A) A guaranteed investment contract

B) A stop-loss order

C) Guaranteeing against loss

D) Portfolio insurance

17. Tying, the practice of requiring a client to purchase one product in order to obtain another, is considered:

A) A common practice in the securities industry.

B) Illegal or unethical in most circumstances.

C) A form of diversification.

D) A type of hedging strategy.

18. The practice of brokers using their own accounts to acquire shares of a new issue before offering it to clients is known as:

A) Allocation

B) Scalping

C) Flipping

D) Laddering

19. Laddering in the context of securities issuance refers to:

A) The illegal practice of submitting fake bids in an IPO to give the impression of high demand.

B) A bond investment strategy that staggers maturity dates.

C) A method of gradually buying into a position to average down the cost.

D) Setting up a sequence of limit orders at incrementally higher prices.

20. The practice of selling securities that one does not own or has not confirmed can be borrowed for delivery is known as:

A) Short selling

B) Naked short selling

C) Put option

D) Call option

21. The act of consolidating orders from different clients into one block to execute a single trade is known as:

A) Block trading

B) Batch processing

C) Bulk buying

D) Aggregation

22. Free-riding refers to:

A) Taking advantage of free research reports without making trades.

B) Selling securities bought with unsettled funds without covering the initial purchase.

C) Utilizing free trading platforms to execute large volumes of trades.

D) Riding the momentum of a stock without analyzing its fundamentals.

23. What is the primary concern with "quote stuffing" in electronic trading?

A) It provides accurate market data.

B) It involves placing a large number of orders and then canceling them to slow down competitors.

C) It ensures liquidity in the market.

D) It is a strategy for long-term investment.

24. The practice of "momentum ignition" refers to:

A) Starting a trend by executing a series of transactions to create the appearance of rapid market movement.

B) Slowing down market momentum through large sell orders.

C) Investing in momentum stocks for long-term gains.

D) Using technical analysis to predict future market movements.

25. What does "blue sheeting" refer to in the context of securities regulation?

A) The process of decorating the trading floor with blue sheets to signal a bullish market.

B) A request by regulatory authorities for detailed trades information to investigate trading activity.

C) The practice of issuing blue-colored stocks.

D) A method of tracking the performance of blue-chip stocks.

26. The act of "back running" involves:

A) Trading ahead of a client's transaction to benefit from the anticipated market impact.

B) Copying the back-office operations of successful firms.

C) Running algorithmic trading strategies in the background.

D) Reversing transactions at the end of the trading day.

27. "Interpositioning" occurs when:

A) A broker unnecessarily inserts an intermediary in a transaction to generate additional fees.

B) Positions in the market are interchanged rapidly.

C) Securities are positioned between different market levels.

D) A broker positions themselves between two clients to facilitate a trade.

28. The practice of "pooling" in securities markets is considered prohibited when it involves:

A) Combining resources for investment purposes in a legal and transparent manner.

B) Creating a secret agreement among traders to manipulate stock prices.

C) Pooling funds to invest in mutual funds or ETFs.

D) Sharing investment strategies among a group of investors.

29. "Benchmark manipulation" refers to:

A) Adjusting a portfolio to match a benchmark index.

B) Manipulating financial benchmarks or indices to benefit derivative positions.

C) Setting performance benchmarks for mutual funds.

D) Using benchmarks to measure the performance of securities.

30. Engaging in "cross trading" is prohibited when it:

A) Involves the buying and selling of securities between clients without actual change in ownership.

B) Is used to provide liquidity in the market.

C) Occurs between two unrelated parties at market price.

D) Is executed to fulfill large orders without impacting the market.

31. "Circular trading" is a form of market manipulation where:

A) Trades are executed in a circular pattern to confuse other market participants.

B) A group of traders buy and sell securities among themselves to create artificial trading volume.

C) Investors use circular logic to justify their trading decisions.

D) Trading occurs in cycles based on market trends.

32. The unethical practice of "banging the close" involves:

A) Celebrating profitable trading days with loud noises.

B) Executing a flurry of trades just before the market close to influence the closing price.

C) Closing all open positions at the end of the trading day.

D) Knocking on the exchange's door to be let in after hours.

33. "Pre-arranged trading" in the context of securities markets usually refers to:

A) Setting up trades between parties at predetermined prices, which may not reflect the current market price.

B) Arranging trades in advance to ensure execution at the opening bell.

C) Planning trading strategies before the market opens.

D) Arranging for trades to be executed automatically through a trading platform.

34. The act of "spoofing" is specifically designed to:

A) Provide humor in the trading environment.

B) Influence the price of a security by placing orders with no intention of executing them.

C) Spoof or mimic the trading strategies of successful traders.

D) Create fake trading accounts for the purpose of testing trading strategies.

35. "Layering" in trading is problematic because it:

A) Adds multiple layers of security to trading accounts.

B) Involves submitting and canceling orders to mislead participants about market demand.

C) Is a strategy for building a diversified investment portfolio.

D) Refers to the layering of fees on investment products.

36. The use of "material non-public information" for trading purposes is prohibited because it:

A) Is considered insider trading, which is illegal and unfair to other market participants.

B) Helps in making informed investment decisions.

C) Is a common practice among professional traders.

D) Ensures that all traders have access to the same information.

37. "Matched orders," where a trader coordinates buy and sell orders of the same size at the same time, are considered manipulative because they:

A) Match the market's demand and supply perfectly.

B) Create a false appearance of trading activity without actual change in ownership.

C) Are used to match buyers with sellers in illiquid markets.

D) Help in maintaining market stability.

38. The practice of "flipping" IPO shares refers to:

A) The gymnastic routine traders perform to celebrate a successful IPO.

B) Buying shares at the IPO price and selling them quickly after trading begins to profit from price jumps.

C) Rotating IPO shares among different accounts to avoid detection.

D) Holding IPO shares long-term to benefit from the company's growth.

39. "Cornering the market" involves:

A) Taking a position in a corner office to better observe market movements.

B) Acquiring sufficient shares of a particular security to control its price.

C) Trading from the corners of the trading floor for better access.

D) Establishing trading desks in the corners of major financial districts.

40. The act of "rumormongering" in the context of trading involves:

A) Sharing verified information about securities.

B) Spreading unverified or false information to influence security prices.

C) Gathering rumors to make trading decisions.

D) Ignoring market rumors to focus on fundamental analysis.

41. "Straw man" transactions in the securities industry refer to:

A) Using a third party to conceal the true party in interest in a transaction.

B) Building a straw man argument to justify investment choices.

C) A type of transaction that is easily defeated or bypassed.

D) Transactions that are considered too weak to be profitable.

42. The practice of "window dressing" by investment managers involves:

A) Decorating their offices to impress clients.

B) Making cosmetic changes to a portfolio before reporting periods to improve its appearance.

C) Adjusting the transparency of portfolio holdings.

D) Changing the portfolio's strategy to match market trends.

43. "Piggybacking" in trading refers to:

A) Following the trades of successful investors without independent analysis.

B) Carrying out trades on the back of market momentum.

C) Trading securities while physically carrying another person.

D) Using leverage to increase the size of trades.

44. The unethical practice of "libel" in the securities market involves:

A) Publishing false statements about a company to manipulate its stock price.

B) Legal action taken against market manipulators.

C) Writing biased research reports without disclosing conflicts of interest.

D) The act of publicly supporting a security while secretly selling it.

Overview of the Regulatory Framework
REGULATORY AGENCIES

1. Which agency is the primary regulator of the U.S. securities markets?

A) Federal Reserve

B) Securities and Exchange Commission (SEC)

C) Financial Industry Regulatory Authority (FINRA)

D) Commodity Futures Trading Commission (CFTC)

2. The Financial Industry Regulatory Authority (FINRA) primarily oversees:

A) Banks

B) Broker-dealers and registered representatives

C) Insurance companies

D) Pension funds

3. What is the role of the Securities Investor Protection Corporation (SIPC)?

A) To insure investors against market losses

B) To protect investors from broker-dealer bankruptcy

C) To regulate stock exchanges

D) To provide educational resources to investors

4. The Commodity Futures Trading Commission (CFTC) regulates:

A) Stock trading

B) Futures and options markets

C) Banking operations

D) Mutual funds

5. Which entity is responsible for enforcing federal securities laws?

A) The Federal Reserve

B) The U.S. Treasury

C) The Securities and Exchange Commission (SEC)

D) The Financial Industry Regulatory Authority (FINRA)

6. The National Association of Securities Dealers (NASD) merged with NYSE Regulation to form:

A) The Securities and Exchange Commission (SEC)

B) The Financial Industry Regulatory Authority (FINRA)

C) The Commodity Futures Trading Commission (CFTC)

D) The Office of the Comptroller of the Currency (OCC)

7. State securities regulators are primarily responsible for:

A) Regulating national securities exchanges

B) Overseeing state-chartered banks

C) Enforcing state securities laws and regulations

D) Managing state pension funds

8. The Office of the Comptroller of the Currency (OCC) regulates:

A) All U.S. banks

B) Federal savings associations and national banks

C) Broker-dealers

D) Credit unions

9. The Municipal Securities Rulemaking Board (MSRB) regulates:

A) Municipal bond issuers

B) The trading of municipal securities

C) Stock exchanges

D) Futures markets

10. Who is responsible for regulating investment advisers?

A) The Federal Reserve

B) The Securities and Exchange Commission (SEC) and state regulators

C) The Financial Industry Regulatory Authority (FINRA)

D) The Commodity Futures Trading Commission (CFTC)

11. The primary function of the Public Company Accounting Oversight Board (PCAOB) is to:

A) Oversee the audits of public companies

B) Regulate public accounting firms

C) Set accounting standards for public companies

D) Both A and B

12. The Federal Deposit Insurance Corporation (FDIC) insures:

A) Stock investments

B) Deposits in banks and thrift institutions

C) Futures contracts

D) Mutual funds

13. The Securities and Exchange Commission (SEC) was established as a result of which legislation?

A) The Dodd-Frank Wall Street Reform and Consumer Protection Act

B) The Sarbanes-Oxley Act

C) The Securities Act of 1933

D) The Securities Exchange Act of 1934

14. The role of the Consumer Financial Protection Bureau (CFPB) is to:

A) Protect consumers from unfair, deceptive, or abusive practices in financial services

B) Regulate securities exchanges

C) Insure bank deposits

D) Oversee the trading of commodities and futures

15. The Financial Crimes Enforcement Network (FinCEN) is a bureau of:

A) The U.S. Department of the Treasury

B) The Securities and Exchange Commission (SEC)

C) The Federal Reserve

D) The Financial Industry Regulatory Authority (FINRA)

16. The North American Securities Administrators Association (NASAA) consists of:

A) Securities regulators from the 50 states, the District of Columbia, and U.S. territories

B) Members from the SEC, FINRA, and CFTC

C) Representatives from major stock exchanges

D) International securities regulators

17. The primary purpose of the Federal Reserve in the context of securities regulation is to:

A) Insure bank deposits

B) Oversee monetary policy and regulate banks

C) Regulate the trading of securities

D) Protect investors from fraud

18. The Jumpstart Our Business Startups (JOBS) Act is enforced by:

A) The U.S. Department of Labor

B) The Securities and Exchange Commission (SEC)

C) The Financial Industry Regulatory Authority (FINRA)

D) State securities regulators

19. The role of the National Futures Association (NFA) is to:

A) Regulate national banks

B) Oversee futures markets and protect investors

C) Insure futures contracts

D) Set interest rates

20. The Investment Company Act of 1940 primarily regulates:

A) Investment advisers

B) Mutual funds and other investment companies

C) Broker-dealers

D) Publicly traded companies

21. The Financial Stability Oversight Council (FSOC) was created to:

A) Identify risks to the financial stability of the United States

B) Oversee the trading of securities

C) Regulate mutual funds

D) Insure bank deposits

22. The primary focus of the International Organization of Securities Commissions (IOSCO) is to:

A) Coordinate global securities regulation

B) Regulate U.S. securities markets

C) Oversee international banking operations

D) Set accounting standards

23. What is the primary purpose of FINRA's Code of Conduct?

A) To outline the ethical standards for trading commodities

B) To set forth the professional conduct standards for broker-dealers and registered representatives

C) To regulate the conduct of investment advisors

D) To establish guidelines for the behavior of corporate executives

24. A broker-dealer's failure to adhere to the "Know Your Customer" (KYC) rules can result in:

A) Increased market volatility

B) Sanctions from the International Organization of Securities Commissions (IOSCO)

C) Disciplinary actions by FINRA or the SEC

D) Mandatory dissolution of the broker-dealer

25. The requirement for broker-dealers to maintain a high standard of commercial honor and just and equitable principles of trade is outlined in:

A) The Sarbanes-Oxley Act

B) FINRA Rule 2010

C) The Dodd-Frank Act

D) The Securities Act of 1933

26. Suitability obligations under FINRA rules require that a broker-dealer:

A) Only recommend investments that are suitable for the client based on their financial situation and risk tolerance

B) Offer the lowest commission rates

C) Provide clients with the highest possible returns

D) Ensure that all investments are insured

27. The practice of excessive trading in a client's account to generate commissions, known as churning, violates which FINRA rule?

A) Rule 2111 (Suitability)

B) Rule 2010 (Standards of Commercial Honor and Principles of Trade)

C) Rule 3310 (Anti-Money Laundering Compliance Program)

D) Both A and B

28. The SEC Rule 15c3-1, known as the "Net Capital Rule," is designed to ensure that:

A) Broker-dealers maintain sufficient liquidity to meet obligations to clients

B) Investments are suitable for clients

C) Securities are priced fairly in the market

D) Broker-dealers achieve a minimum level of profitability

29. The Anti-Money Laundering (AML) rules require broker-dealers to:

A) Conduct background checks on all new clients

B) Report suspicious transactions exceeding $5,000 to the Financial Crimes Enforcement Network (FinCEN)

C) Ensure all employees are certified financial analysts

D) Only deal in government securities

30. Regulation Best Interest (Reg BI), established by the SEC, requires broker-dealers to:

A) Act in the best interest of their retail customers when making a recommendation

B) Offer the best commission rates in the industry

C) Invest primarily in interest-bearing securities

D) Disclose all conflicts of interest in their annual reports

31. The primary function of the Office of Compliance Inspections and Examinations (OCIE) is to:

A) Provide compliance resources to small firms

B) Conduct examinations of SEC-regulated entities to ensure compliance with the law

C) Oversee the compliance of non-profit organizations with federal securities laws

D) Inspect foreign broker-dealers for compliance with U.S. regulations

32. FINRA Rule 3220, the "Gift Rule," limits the value of gifts given by members to:

A) $100 per person per year

B) $500 per person per year

C) $1000 per person per year

D) There is no specific limit, as long as it's reasonable

33. The "Taping Rule" (FINRA Rule 3170) requires certain broker-dealers to:

A) Record all telephone conversations with clients

B) Use tape backups for all digital records

C) Tape all meetings and conversations in the office for security purposes

D) Record conversations with clients suspected of illegal activities

34. The SEC's Regulation Fair Disclosure (Reg FD) is aimed at:

A) Preventing insider trading by requiring the fair disclosure of material information to all investors at the same time

B) Ensuring that all broker-dealers disclose their fees upfront

C) Mandating that mutual funds disclose their investment strategies

D) Requiring fair treatment of all clients, regardless of account size

35. The Consolidated Audit Trail (CAT) initiative requires broker-dealers to:

A) Consolidate all client audits into a single annual report

B) Report certain transactions and order events to a central repository

C) Audit their compliance with the Net Capital Rule annually

D) Keep a consolidated log of all trades made by the firm

36. Under FINRA Rule 4512, member firms must make a reasonable effort to obtain information about:

A) The political contributions of their clients

B) The investment experience, financial status, and age of their clients

C) The educational background of their clients

D) The employment history of their clients for the past five years

37. The purpose of the "Customer Identification Program" (CIP) as part of AML compliance is to:

A) Identify high-net-worth clients for premium services

B) Verify the identity of clients opening an account

C) Ensure that clients are not politically exposed persons

D) Identify clients with a history of market manipulation

38. Broker-dealers are required to provide a "Customer Relationship Summary" (Form CRS) to retail investors to:

A) Summarize the services offered and the fees charged

B) Provide a summary of the broker-dealer's investment strategies

C) Outline the historical performance of the broker-dealer's investments

D) Provide a biography of each broker at the firm

39. The "Limit Order Display Rule" under the SEC's Regulation NMS requires that:

A) All limit orders be executed immediately

B) Broker-dealers must display certain limit orders to the public

C) Clients must limit the number of orders placed per day

D) Limit orders must be approved by a compliance officer before submission

40. The "Know Your Product" (KYP) requirements mandate that broker-dealers:

A) Understand and communicate the risks and rewards of the products they recommend

B) Know the manufacturing process of the products they invest in

C) Have a personal experience with every product before recommending it

D) Keep a detailed inventory of all products sold in the last fiscal year

41. The SEC's "Order Protection Rule" is designed to:

A) Protect orders from being lost in the system

B) Ensure that trades are executed at the best available price

C) Prevent unauthorized orders from being placed

D) Protect the order information of high-profile clients

42. The "Large Trader Reporting Rule" requires:

A) All traders to report any trade over $10,000

B) Traders who conduct a substantial amount of trading activity to identify themselves to the SEC

C) Daily reporting of all trades made by a firm

D) Reporting of trades only in the event of an audit

43. FINRA's "Conflict of Interest Rule" requires firms to:

A) Avoid all conflicts of interest in their business practices

B) Manage and disclose conflicts of interest related to the allocation of investment opportunities among clients

C) Only hire employees who have no potential conflicts of interest

D) Ensure that all employees sign a conflict of interest statement annually

44. The "Market Access Rule" (Rule 15c3-5) under the SEC requires that:

A) All investors have equal access to the markets

B) Broker-dealers that provide clients with access to the market maintain risk management controls

C) Markets are accessible 24/7

D) Foreign markets comply with U.S. market access standards

MEMBER CONDUCT

----

1. What is the primary goal of establishing rules for member conduct within the securities industry?

A) To ensure market stability

B) To maximize the profits of financial firms

C) To protect investors and maintain fair, orderly, and efficient markets

D) To limit the number of new entrants into the market

2. Which rule requires brokers to make recommendations that are suitable for their clients based on the client's financial situation and needs?

A) The Best Interest Rule

B) The Know Your Customer (KYC) Rule

C) The Suitability Rule

D) The Fair Dealing Rule

3. What does the term "churning" refer to in the context of member conduct?

A) The process of transferring securities between accounts to diversify a portfolio

B) Excessive trading in a client's account primarily to generate commissions

C) The use of complex algorithms to trade securities rapidly

D) Rotating between different asset classes to take advantage of market conditions

4. Which FINRA rule is designed to prevent conflicts of interest in the allocation of new issues?

A) The Public Offering Rule

B) The Spinning Rule

C) The IPO Allocation Rule

D) The Fair Access Rule

5. The practice of "front running" is prohibited because it:

A) Ensures that all clients receive the same information at the same time

B) Involves executing a broker's personal trades before client trades

C) Is a method of securing the best possible price for clients

D) Encourages diversification of client portfolios

6. Under FINRA regulations, what is required of a broker when opening a new account for a customer?

A) Obtain written approval from the SEC

B) Verify the customer's identity and assess their investment profile

C) Invest the customer's funds in a default money market fund

D) Provide the customer with a list of the top-performing stocks

7. The "Taping Rule" requires firms to record phone conversations to:

A) Monitor the quality of customer service

B) Ensure compliance with trading and sales communications regulations

C) Provide training material for new employees

D) Create a database of customer complaints

8. Regulation Best Interest (Reg BI) obligates brokers to:

A) Only recommend investments with the highest returns

B) Act in the best interest of their retail customers when making a recommendation

C) Disclose their commission rates upfront

D) Guarantee the performance of recommended investments

9. A broker's failure to disclose material information to a client can be classified as:

A) An acceptable practice in certain markets

B) A minor violation if the investment performs well

C) A breach of the fiduciary duty

D) Misrepresentation or omission of facts

10. The prohibition against "selling away" is designed to prevent:

A) The sale of securities not held in inventory by the broker-dealer

B) Brokers from selling securities during a market downturn

C) Unauthorized transactions not supervised by the broker's firm

D) The sale of securities directly by issuers to investors

11. What is the purpose of Anti-Money Laundering (AML) compliance programs within brokerage firms?

A) To ensure that all employees are paid fairly

B) To detect and report potentially suspicious financial transactions

C) To monitor the personal trading activities of employees

D) To prevent insider trading

12. The requirement for firms to adopt a written Customer Identification Program (CIP) is part of:

A) The Dodd-Frank Wall Street Reform

B) The USA PATRIOT Act

C) The Sarbanes-Oxley Act

D) The Securities Act of 1933

13. Which of the following is considered a manipulative or deceptive practice under securities law?

A) Diversifying a client's investment portfolio

B) Using client testimonials in advertising without disclosure

C) Marking the close

D) Periodic rebalancing of a mutual fund

14. The duty to provide "best execution" for client trades means:

A) Executing trades at the highest possible price

B) Ensuring trades are executed in a timely manner and at the best available price

C) Trading exclusively on major exchanges

D) Prioritizing institutional orders over retail orders

15. What does the "Fair Dealing with Customers" principle require of securities professionals?

A) To engage in high-frequency trading

B) To ensure that all communications with customers are clear, fair, and not misleading

C) To deal with customers only during official market hours

D) To offer the same investment opportunities to all customers regardless of their investment experience

16. The prohibition of "market manipulation" includes practices such as:

A) Asset allocation

B) Pump and dump schemes

C) Long-term investing

D) Diversification

17. A broker's use of "discretionary authority" in a client's account without written authorization is:

A) Required for all accounts

B) Permitted only in margin accounts

C) A violation of FINRA rules

D) Allowed if the broker has known the client for more than a year

18. The "Know Your Product" (KYP) requirement obligates brokers to:

A) Invest personally in the products they recommend

B) Understand the risks, rewards, and costs associated with the products they recommend

C) Recommend only products that are proprietary to their firm

D) Focus on products with the highest commission rates

19. The SEC's "Order Protection Rule" aims to:

A) Prevent brokers from executing orders

B) Ensure that investors receive the best price execution for their orders

C) Limit the number of orders placed by a single investor

D) Protect orders from being intercepted by third parties

20. The practice of "wash trading," where a trader buys and sells securities for the purpose of generating activity and influencing the price, is:

A) A recommended strategy for day traders

B) Prohibited as it creates a misleading appearance of market activity

C) Allowed under certain conditions to provide liquidity

D) Encouraged to test market resilience

21. What is the significance of the "Customer Relationship Summary" (Form CRS) that broker-dealers must provide to retail investors?

A) It summarizes the investor's rights under the Securities Investor Protection Act

B) It provides detailed biographies of the firm's brokers

C) It outlines the nature of the relationship, including fees, services, and conflicts of interest

D) It guarantees a minimum return on investments

22. The requirement for continuous and rigorous supervision of the trading activities of registered representatives is aimed at:

A) Increasing the profitability of brokerage firms

B) Ensuring compliance with market regulations and protecting investor interests

C) Reducing the number of transactions to manage risk

D) Monitoring the personal trading activities of employees for tax purposes

23. What is the primary purpose of a firm's compliance program under securities regulation?

A) To ensure the firm maximizes its profits

B) To monitor and enforce adherence to all applicable securities laws and regulations

C) To manage the firm's marketing strategies

D) To track the performance of the firm's investments

24. An effective Anti-Money Laundering (AML) program must include:

A) Annual picnics for employees

B) Procedures for detecting and reporting suspicious activities

C) A policy against investing in technology stocks

D) Mandatory profit-sharing with clients

25. The Securities and Exchange Commission (SEC) requires that firms adhere to Regulation S-P for:

A) Sharing profits with shareholders

B) Protecting customers' privacy and safeguarding their confidential information

C) Speculating on securities prices

D) Distributing dividends on preferred stocks

26. Which of the following is a requirement under the Sarbanes-Oxley Act for public companies?

A) CEOs and CFOs must certify the accuracy of financial statements

B) All employees must hold a finance degree

C) Companies must disclose their political contributions

D) Firms are required to trade only in OTC markets

27. The primary goal of Business Continuity Plans (BCP) is to:

A) Ensure firms have a strategy for maintaining operations during significant disruptions

B) Guarantee a fixed return on investments during economic downturns

C) Monitor employee behavior on social media

D) Ensure all trades are executed within milliseconds

28. Cybersecurity regulations in the securities industry are designed to:

A) Limit the use of electronic trading platforms

B) Protect firms from paying taxes

C) Safeguard firms' and clients' digital information from unauthorized access or attacks

D) Encourage the use of paper records over digital ones

29. The "Know Your Customer" (KYC) rules are primarily intended to:

A) Ensure that customers are knowledgeable about the stock market

B) Verify the identity of clients and assess the suitability of investments

C) Guarantee that customers always make profitable investments

D) Encourage customers to trade more frequently

30. Regulation Fair Disclosure (Reg FD) aims to:

A) Ensure all investors have equal access to material company information

B) Discourage companies from making any public disclosures

C) Allow insiders to trade based on non-public information

D) Make financial reporting optional for public companies

31. The role of a firm's Chief Compliance Officer (CCO) is to:

A) Manage the firm's investment strategies

B) Oversee and enforce the firm's adherence to legal and regulatory compliance requirements

C) Handle the firm's public relations

D) Direct the firm's sales strategies

32. The Financial Industry Regulatory Authority (FINRA) requires that member firms create and maintain a Written Supervisory Procedures (WSP) manual to:

A) Detail the firm's holiday schedule

B) Outline the supervisory structure and procedures for monitoring compliance with FINRA rules

C) Describe the firm's dress code

D) List the firm's preferred vendors and suppliers

33. The requirement for periodic compliance training for employees is to:

A) Ensure that employees remain competitive in fantasy sports leagues

B) Keep employees informed about changes in securities laws and firm policies

C) Discourage employees from taking vacations

D) Increase the firm's operational costs

34. The use of Restricted Lists by brokerage firms is to:

A) Keep track of employees' birthdays

B) Prevent conflicts of interest by restricting trading in certain securities

C) Limit the number of clients a broker can have

D) Restrict employees from using social media

35. The purpose of the Office of the Whistleblower within the SEC is to:

A) Provide entertainment at corporate events

B) Encourage the reporting of securities law violations by offering protections and incentives

C) Discourage employees from reporting misconduct

D) Monitor the personal lives of employees

36. A firm's obligation to conduct due diligence on new products before offering them to clients is to:

A) Ensure the products are entertaining

B) Verify that the products meet legal and regulatory standards and are suitable for clients

C) Confirm that the products can be sold at a discount

D) Ensure that the products have been featured in financial news outlets

37. The concept of "Material Nonpublic Information" (MNPI) is crucial in preventing:

A) Over-diversification of investments

B) Insider trading

C) Excessive use of leverage

D) High-frequency trading

38. The SEC's Consolidated Audit Trail (CAT) system is designed to:

A) Track the sale of all books and records related to securities transactions

B) Provide a comprehensive database of all securities transactions to enhance market surveillance

C) Limit the number of transactions an individual can make

D) Audit the personal financial transactions of all employees in the securities industry

39. The requirement for firms to maintain accurate books and records under the Securities Exchange Act of 1934 is to:

A) Ensure that firms can accurately calculate their taxes

B) Facilitate the review and examination of a firm's business activities by regulators

C) Discourage firms from using electronic databases

D) Make financial analysis more challenging

40. The "Customer Complaint Rule" requires firms to:

A) Ignore complaints that are deemed insignificant

B) Record and address all written complaints received from customers

C) Only respond to complaints received via email

D) Share customer complaints with competitors

41. The practice of "marking the close" is prohibited because it:

A) Encourages long-term investment strategies

B) Involves manipulating the price of a security at the close of the market to benefit certain positions

C) Is a necessary part of daily trading activities

D) Helps in accurately determining the market closing price

42. The "Net Capital Rule" is intended to ensure that:

A) Firms have enough capital to engage in day trading

B) Broker-dealers maintain a cushion of liquidity sufficient to cover obligations to customers

C) Firms allocate capital to the most profitable sectors

D) All investments made by the firm are fully insured

43. The role of Self-Regulatory Organizations (SROs) like FINRA in the securities industry is to:

A) Provide networking opportunities for finance professionals

B) Regulate member brokerage firms and exchange markets to enforce federal securities laws

C) Offer investment advice to retail investors

D) Compete with the SEC in regulatory authority

44. The "Order Audit Trail System" (OATS) requirements help regulators:

A) Predict market trends

B) Track the lifecycle of orders to ensure market integrity and investigate potential violations

C) Encourage the use of algorithmic trading

D) Monitor the lunch orders of traders to ensure dietary compliance

COMPLIANCE CONSIDERATIONS

1. What is the primary goal of compliance programs within financial institutions?

A) To ensure profitability

B) To monitor and enforce adherence to laws and regulations

C) To manage employee benefits

D) To oversee marketing strategies

2. Which of the following is a key component of an Anti-Money Laundering (AML) compliance program?

A) Customer entertainment policies

B) Procedures for detecting and reporting suspicious activity

C) Investment return guarantees

D) Social media monitoring guidelines

3. Regulation S-P is concerned with:

A) Sportsmanship among traders

B) The speed of trade executions

C) Protecting customers' privacy and safeguarding their confidential information

D) Setting performance benchmarks for securities

4. Under the Sarbanes-Oxley Act, who must certify the accuracy of financial reports?

A) The head of sales

B) The Chief Technology Officer

C) The CEO and CFO

D) All employees

5. The purpose of a Business Continuity Plan (BCP) is to:

A) Ensure uninterrupted social events in the workplace

B) Guarantee a fixed return on investments

C) Provide a strategy for the firm to continue operations under adverse conditions

D) Monitor competitors' business strategies

6. Cybersecurity regulations in the securities industry aim to:

A) Encourage the use of fax machines over email

B) Protect against unauthorized access to digital information

C) Limit the use of mobile trading apps

D) Promote paper record-keeping

7. The "Know Your Customer" (KYC) rules are designed to:

A) Ensure customers are familiar with the stock market

B) Verify the identity of clients and assess the suitability of investments

C) Encourage customers to engage in day trading

D) Collect feedback on customer service

8. Regulation Fair Disclosure (Reg FD) is intended to:

A) Encourage companies to hold information closely

B) Ensure all investors have equal access to material company information

C) Allow selective disclosure to favored investors

D) Discourage public companies from issuing earnings forecasts

9. The Chief Compliance Officer (CCO) is responsible for:

A) Directing the company's investment strategies

B) Enforcing adherence to legal and regulatory standards

C) Managing the company's social media profiles

D) Overseeing the company's hiring process

10. Written Supervisory Procedures (WSP) are required to:

A) Detail the company's dress code

B) Outline the supervisory structure and procedures for compliance

C) List the company's holiday schedule

D) Describe the company's product offerings

11. Periodic compliance training for employees is important because it:

A) Helps employees prepare for performance reviews

B) Keeps employees informed about regulatory changes and company policies

C) Is a requirement for employee promotion

D) Reduces the need for supervisory oversight

12. The use of Restricted Lists in securities firms is primarily to:

A) Track employees' birthdays and work anniversaries

B) Prevent conflicts of interest by restricting trading in certain securities

C) Limit the number of clients a broker can have

D) Restrict employees from accessing certain areas of the office

13. The Office of the Whistleblower within the SEC was established to:

A) Organize team-building activities

B) Encourage reporting of securities law violations by offering protections and incentives

C) Discourage employees from reporting unethical behavior

D) Track employee complaints about management

14. Due diligence on new products is necessary to:

A) Ensure the products are entertaining

B) Verify that products meet legal and regulatory standards and are suitable for clients

C) Confirm that products can be sold at a discount

D) Ensure products have been advertised on television

15. The concept of "Material Nonpublic Information" (MNPI) is crucial for preventing:

A) Diversification of investment portfolios

B) Insider trading

C) The use of leverage in investment strategies

D) The practice of day trading

16. The Consolidated Audit Trail (CAT) system was developed to:

A) Track the personal transactions of all employees in the securities industry

B) Provide a comprehensive database of securities transactions for market surveillance

C) Limit the number of transactions an individual can make

D) Audit the financial transactions of celebrities

17. Maintaining accurate books and records is crucial for firms because it:

A) Helps in preparing for tax season

B) Facilitates regulatory review and examination of the firm's business activities

C) Makes it easier to calculate employee bonuses

D) Is only a suggestion, not a requirement

18. The "Customer Complaint Rule" mandates that firms:

A) Keep all customer complaints confidential and not act on them

B) Record and address all written complaints received from customers

C) Only respond to complaints that are submitted via certified mail

D) Forward all complaints to the SEC without review

19. "Marking the close" is prohibited because it:

A) Is a necessary part of daily trading activities

B) Helps in accurately determining the market closing price

C) Involves manipulating the price of a security at the close of the market

D) Encourages long-term investment strategies

20. The "Net Capital Rule" ensures that:

A) Firms can engage in proprietary trading without restrictions

B) Broker-dealers maintain sufficient liquidity to meet obligations to customers

C) Firms allocate capital to the most profitable sectors

D) All investments made by the firm are fully insured

21. Self-Regulatory Organizations (SROs) like FINRA play a role in the securities industry by:

A) Providing networking opportunities for finance professionals

B) Regulating member brokerage firms and exchange markets

C) Offering investment advice to retail investors

D) Competing with the SEC for regulatory authority

22. The "Order Audit Trail System" (OATS) helps regulators:

A) Predict market trends based on lunch orders

B) Track the lifecycle of orders to ensure market integrity

C) Encourage the use of algorithmic trading strategies

D) Monitor the dietary habits of traders for health studies

23. Which regulation requires firms to adopt comprehensive policies and procedures to protect customer information from cybersecurity threats?

A) Regulation S-ID

B) Regulation S-P

C) FINRA Rule 3110

D) SEC Rule 206(4)-7

24. The process of "layering" or "spoofing" in trading activities is considered:

A) A legitimate strategy for market makers

B) An acceptable form of high-frequency trading

C) A manipulative trading practice

D) A recommended technique for day traders

25. For a firm to meet its compliance with the "Market Access Rule" (Rule 15c3-5), it must:

A) Provide direct market access to all clients

B) Establish risk management controls and supervisory procedures

C) Offer the lowest transaction costs in the market

D) Guarantee the execution of all trades

26. The primary purpose of the "Customer Identification Program" (CIP) is to:

A) Ensure all customers are profitable

B) Identify potential insider trading activities

C) Verify the identity of individuals opening accounts

D) Monitor the trading habits of high-net-worth individuals

27. Regulation BI (Best Interest) applies to:

A) All financial transactions globally

B) Recommendations made by broker-dealers to retail customers

C) Banking institutions' lending practices

D) Insurance companies' policy offerings

28. The "Fiduciary Rule," as proposed by the Department of Labor, primarily affects:

A) All employees within a firm

B) Brokers and advisors providing retirement advice

C) Accountants and auditors

D) Legal advisors

29. Which of the following is a requirement under FINRA Rule 4512 (Customer Account Information)?

A) Recording the political affiliations of clients

B) Obtaining a client's employment history for the past 10 years

C) Keeping accurate and updated customer account information

D) Verifying the social media profiles of clients

30. The SEC's "Regulation SCI" (Systems Compliance and Integrity) focuses on:

A) Social media compliance

B) Ensuring that market participants' technological systems are resilient and compliant

C) The integrity of manual trading systems

D) Compliance with international trading standards

31. "Wash sales" are prohibited because they:

A) Create artificial trading volume without actual change in ownership

B) Are a form of high-frequency trading

C) Involve the physical exchange of securities

D) Are used to launder money

32. The primary objective of the "Patriot Act" in the financial industry is to:

A) Promote patriotic investments

B) Enhance cybersecurity measures

C) Prevent money laundering and terrorist financing

D) Regulate international trade agreements

33. A "Chinese Wall" within a financial institution is intended to:

A) Promote communication between different departments

B) Prevent the spread of confidential information across different areas of the firm

C) Encourage collaboration on investment banking deals

D) Isolate the firm from international markets

34. The "Blue Sky Laws" are designed to:

A) Regulate aviation investments

B) Protect investors from securities fraud at the state level

C) Govern maritime trading practices

D) Standardize accounting practices across states

35. Under FINRA's Rule 2210 (Communications with the Public), which of the following is true?

A) Firms can guarantee future performance in their advertisements

B) All communications must be fair, balanced, and not misleading

C) Only negative customer testimonials are allowed

D) Firms are encouraged to use complex jargon in retail communications

36. The "Tick Size Pilot Program" was introduced to:

A) Decrease the speed of electronic trading

B) Test the impact of wider tick sizes on small-cap stocks

C) Increase the minimum price variation for all stocks

D) Eliminate decimal pricing in stock trading

37. "Soft Dollars" practices involve:

A) The use of client brokerage commissions to purchase research and services

B) Direct cash payments for securities transactions

C) Exchange of goods without involving financial transactions

D) Trading in foreign currencies at discounted rates

38. The "Volcker Rule" primarily aims to:

A) Allow banks to engage in proprietary trading without restrictions

B) Prevent banks from making speculative investments that do not benefit their customers

C) Encourage banks to invest in hedge funds and private equity funds

D) Increase the liquidity of the banking sector

39. The "TRACE" (Trade Reporting and Compliance Engine) system is used to:

A) Track the execution speed of trades

B) Report transactions in eligible fixed income securities

C) Monitor the personal trades of employees

D) Ensure compliance with global trading regulations

40. The "Global Investment Performance Standards" (GIPS) are:

A) Mandatory regulations set by the SEC

B) Ethical standards for presenting investment performance

C) Guidelines for cryptocurrency investments

D) Federal laws governing international trade

41. The "Liquidity Coverage Ratio" (LCR) requirement under Basel III aims to ensure that:

A) Banks have an adequate level of unencumbered high-quality liquid assets

B) All investments are liquidated at market open

C) Securities firms maintain a fixed ratio of liquid to illiquid assets

D) Hedge funds provide liquidity support to the markets

42. The "Fair Credit Reporting Act" (FCRA) in the financial industry is designed to:

A) Ensure accuracy and privacy of credit information

B) Regulate the use of credit by minors

C) Provide unlimited access to credit reports for financial firms

D) Standardize the calculation of credit scores across industries

43. "Regulation A+" under the JOBS Act allows companies to:

A) Avoid registering with the SEC entirely

B) Offer and sell securities up to a certain threshold without traditional registration

C) Engage in unlimited proprietary trading

D) Bypass state securities laws

44. The "Senior Safe Act" encourages financial professionals to report:

A) Any profitable investments for seniors

B) Suspected cases of elder financial abuse without fear of liability

C) The retirement status of all clients

D) Violations of the minimum investment age requirements

Economic Fundamentals, Investment Strategies, and Market Dynamics

ECONOMIC INDICATORS

1. What does the Gross Domestic Product (GDP) measure?

A) The total corporate profits within a country

B) The total market value of all goods and services produced within a country in a year

C) The total exports of a country

D) The total value of the stock market

2. The Consumer Price Index (CPI) is an indicator of:

A) Stock market performance

B) Inflation or deflation

C) Unemployment rates

D) Government spending

3. Which economic indicator is considered a leading indicator of economic health?

A) GDP

B) CPI

C) Unemployment rate

D) Purchasing Managers' Index (PMI)

4. What does an increase in the Producer Price Index (PPI) typically indicate?

A) Decreased inflation

B) Increased consumer purchasing power

C) Potential for increased inflation

D) A decrease in manufacturing costs

5. The unemployment rate measures:

A) The percentage of the total workforce that is unemployed and actively seeking employment

B) The percentage of the population that is employed

C) The total number of people unemployed

D) The percentage of the total workforce that is employed in the agricultural sector

6. What does a yield curve inversion often indicate about the economy's future?

A) Rapid economic growth

B) A potential recession

C) Stability in the bond market

D) Decreased interest rates

7. The Federal Reserve might raise interest rates in response to:

A) A decrease in the CPI

B) An increase in unemployment

C) Signs of increasing inflation

D) A decrease in GDP

8. What is the significance of the balance of trade in economic analysis?

A) It measures the net earnings from exports and imports

B) It indicates the total value of a country's currency

C) It shows the balance between government spending and revenue

D) It represents the difference between a country's exports and imports

9. Housing starts are a key economic indicator because they reflect:

A) The overall health of the real estate market

B) The profitability of the construction industry

C) Consumer confidence and spending power

D) Both A and C

10. Retail sales figures are important to economists because they:

A) Indicate trends in consumer spending

B) Show the profitability of retail companies

C) Measure the effectiveness of online advertising

D) Predict the future of the stock market

11. The term "stagflation" refers to an economy that is experiencing:

A) High inflation and high unemployment

B) High inflation and rapid growth

C) Low inflation and low unemployment

D) Low inflation and a recession

12. Core CPI differs from CPI by excluding:

A) Housing prices

B) Stock market investments

C) Food and energy prices

D) Government spending

13. A country's "current account" measures:

A) The difference between its savings and investment spending

B) The total value of its currency in circulation

C) Its trade balance, net income from abroad, and net current transfers

D) The government's budget deficit or surplus

14. What does an increase in consumer confidence typically lead to?

A) Decreased spending

B) Increased saving

C) Increased consumer spending

D) A decrease in GDP

15. The "Beige Book" is published by the Federal Reserve to:

A) Detail its monetary policy decisions

B) Provide a summary of economic conditions in each of the Fed's districts

C) Report on the state of the banking sector

D) Announce changes in interest rates

16. The Non-Farm Payroll report is significant because it:

A) Measures the total number of farm animals in the agricultural sector

B) Provides data on the number of jobs added or lost in the economy, excluding farm workers

C) Indicates the profitability of the non-farm sector

D) Measures the productivity of non-farm workers

17. A country experiencing a trade deficit is:

A) Exporting more than it is importing

B) Importing more than it is exporting

C) Maintaining a balanced trade with its trading partners

D) Seeing a decrease in domestic manufacturing

18. The "velocity of money" refers to:

A) The speed at which stock prices change

B) The rate at which money is exchanged in an economy

C) The time it takes for the government to print new money

D) The speed of electronic fund transfers

19. The "Labor Force Participation Rate" measures:

A) The total number of employees in the labor force

B) The percentage of the working-age population that is part of the labor force

C) The growth rate of the labor force

D) The percentage of the labor force that is unemployed

20. An increase in the "Money Supply" typically leads to:

A) Lower interest rates

B) Higher interest rates

C) Increased inflation

D) Both A and C

21. The "Capital to Labor Ratio" is an indicator of:

A) The amount of capital allocated per labor unit in production

B) The profitability of capital investments

C) The efficiency of labor in generating capital

D) The ratio of capital goods prices to wages

22. "Quantitative Easing" is a monetary policy used to:

A) Increase the money supply by purchasing government securities

B) Decrease the national debt

C) Raise interest rates

D) Reduce the money supply

23. Which indicator is used to measure the average change in selling prices received by domestic producers for their output over time?

A) Consumer Confidence Index

B) Producer Price Index (PPI)

C) Gross Domestic Product (GDP)

D) Retail Sales Index

24. The term "real GDP" refers to GDP:

A) Adjusted for inflation

B) Calculated using current market prices

C) Excluding international trade

D) Before taxes

25. What does a high Consumer Confidence Index indicate about the economy?

A) It is likely in a recession

B) Consumers are saving more than spending

C) Consumers feel optimistic about the economy and are likely to spend more

D) The stock market is underperforming

26. An increase in the Federal Funds Rate typically indicates that the Federal Reserve is trying to:

A) Stimulate economic growth

B) Curb inflation

C) Increase unemployment

D) Decrease the value of the dollar

27. The "Beige Book" is published how often by the Federal Reserve?

A) Weekly

B) Monthly

C) Bi-monthly

D) Eight times a year

28. A persistent trade deficit may lead to:

A) A stronger national currency

B) Increased foreign investment

C) Depletion of foreign reserves

D) Lower interest rates

29. The Employment Cost Index (ECI) is significant because it measures:

A) The cost of living in various cities

B) Changes in the costs of employing labor, including wages and benefits

C) The profitability of companies in the employment sector

D) The number of new businesses created in the economy

30. Which of the following best describes "quantitative easing"?

A) Raising interest rates to control inflation

B) The central bank selling government securities to reduce the money supply

C) The central bank purchasing assets to increase the money supply and encourage lending and investment

D) Decreasing government spending to balance the budget

31. The National Debt of a country is:

A) The total amount of money that a country's government has borrowed

B) The amount of money a country owes to foreign investors

C) The total of a country's exports minus its imports

D) The sum of all personal debt within the country

32. What does the term "inflation targeting" refer to?

A) A policy where the central bank sets a specific inflation rate as its goal

B) The process of adjusting interest rates daily to control inflation

C) A fiscal policy aimed at reducing government spending

D) The strategy of increasing taxes to reduce consumer spending

33. Leading Economic Indicators (LEI) are used to:

A) Analyze the historical performance of the economy

B) Predict future economic activity

C) Measure the current level of economic activity

D) Determine the past causes of economic downturns

34. The "Phillips Curve" illustrates the relationship between:

A) Inflation and unemployment

B) Interest rates and inflation

C) GDP growth and inflation

D) Unemployment and GDP growth

35. A country's "fiscal policy" is determined by:

A) Its central bank

B) International trade agreements

C) Its government's budget decisions, including spending and taxation

D) The global economic environment

36. The "money multiplier effect" describes how:

A) An increase in bank deposits can lead to a larger increase in the total money supply

B) Interest rates directly influence the stock market

C) Inflation reduces the real value of money

D) Government spending directly increases GDP

37. "Deflation" is a condition in which:

A) Prices for goods and services increase rapidly

B) The supply of money decreases

C) Prices for goods and services decrease

D) The economy is growing rapidly

38. The "discount rate" is:

A) The interest rate charged to commercial banks and other depository institutions on loans they receive from their regional Federal Reserve Bank's lending facility

B) The rate at which the stock market is expected to grow

C) The interest rate set for interbank loans

D) A fixed rate determined by the national government for all loans

39. A "budget surplus" occurs when:

A) A government's expenditures exceed its revenues

B) A government's revenues exceed its expenditures

C) The national debt is fully paid off

D) A country's GDP growth rate exceeds its inflation rate

40. The "Gini coefficient" is a measure of:

A) A country's economic growth rate

B) The distribution of income across a population

C) The efficiency of a country's labor force

D) The profitability of a country's industries

41. "Crowding out" refers to a situation where:

A) Increased government spending leads to reduced investment by the private sector

B) Private sector investments overshadow government spending initiatives

C) Government policies discourage private investments

D) The government monopolizes certain industries, eliminating private competition

42. The "Purchasing Power Parity" (PPP) theory suggests that:

A) Exchange rates should adjust to equalize the cost of a basket of goods in different countries

B) Stronger currencies always buy more goods than weaker ones

C) Purchasing power is solely determined by GDP

D) Inflation rates are consistent across countries

43. "Capital flight" occurs when:

A) Money rapidly flows into a country to take advantage of high interest rates

B) Large amounts of capital are invested in infrastructure projects

C) Money rapidly leaves a country due to economic or political instability

D) A country's capital city experiences significant population growth

44. The "Twin Deficits" hypothesis relates to a country experiencing:

A) High levels of both inflation and unemployment

B) Deficits in both its trade balance and government budget

C) Deficits in education and healthcare funding

D) A deficit in natural resources and technological advancement

INVESTMENT STRATEGIES

1. What is the primary goal of a diversified investment strategy?

A) To maximize returns by investing in a single asset class

B) To reduce risk by spreading investments across various asset classes

C) To focus solely on bonds for income generation

D) To invest exclusively in emerging markets for high growth

2. Which investment strategy involves buying undervalued stocks in anticipation of their future growth?

A) Short selling

B) Value investing

C) Day trading

D) Arbitrage

3. Growth investing focuses on:

A) Companies that pay high dividends

B) Stocks that are expected to grow at an above-average rate compared to their industry

C) Government bonds

D) Real estate investments

4. What does asset allocation refer to in investment strategy?

A) Choosing specific stocks to buy

B) The process of dividing investments among different kinds of asset classes, such as stocks, bonds, and cash

C) Investing all funds into a single asset for maximum return

D) Allocating assets to only high-risk investments

5. Dollar-cost averaging is a strategy in which an investor:

A) Invests a fixed dollar amount into a particular investment on a regular schedule, regardless of the share price

B) Converts all investments to cash during market downturns

C) Focuses on short-term trading to maximize profits

D) Buys more shares when prices are high and fewer shares when prices are low

6. Which strategy is typically employed by investors seeking to match the returns of a specific benchmark or index?

A) Active management

B) Passive management

C) Fundamental analysis

D) Technical analysis

7. The concept of "buy and hold" strategy is based on the belief that:

A) Short-term market fluctuations can be accurately predicted and exploited

B) Long-term investment offers the potential for significant returns, despite short-term market volatility

C) Investing in commodities is less risky than investing in stocks

D) Bonds should be sold quickly to mitigate interest rate risk

8. What is the main focus of income investing?

A) Achieving capital appreciation

B) Generating regular income from investments, such as dividends from stocks or interest from bonds

C) Speculating on currency fluctuations

D) Investing in technology startups

9. Sector rotation is an investment strategy that involves:

A) Moving investments from one sector to another based on cyclical trends

B) Keeping investments in the same sector regardless of market conditions

C) Investing only in the technology sector

D) Avoiding sectors that are considered volatile

10. In the context of investment strategies, what is "market timing"?

A) Investing the same amount in the market at regular intervals

B) Attempting to predict market highs and lows to buy low and sell high

C) Following a long-term buy and hold strategy without attempting to predict market movements

D) Allocating assets based on a fixed schedule, regardless of market conditions

11. What is the primary characteristic of a "contrarian" investment strategy?

A) Following the current market trends

B) Investing based on popular financial news

C) Going against prevailing market trends

D) Focusing exclusively on bonds

12. Technical analysis in investment strategy involves:

A) Analyzing financial statements to determine a company's value

B) Using historical market data and charts to predict future price movements

C) Interviewing company management to assess future growth potential

D) Focusing on macroeconomic indicators to select investments

13. Risk parity is an investment strategy designed to:

A) Allocate portfolio risk equally among different asset classes

B) Invest only in low-risk securities

C) Concentrate risk in high-growth assets

D) Avoid any form of market risk

14. The "momentum" investment strategy is based on the idea that:

A) Assets that have decreased in price will continue to perform poorly

B) Assets that have performed well in the past will continue to perform well in the future

C) Investments should be sold as soon as they gain any positive momentum

D) Market momentum is irrelevant to investment decisions

15. Which strategy might an investor use to protect against a potential decrease in the value of their stock holdings?

A) Purchasing put options

B) Engaging in high-frequency trading

C) Investing in penny stocks

D) Focusing on international equities

16. ESG investing considers which of the following factors?

A) Entertainment, Sports, and Gaming

B) Environmental, Social, and Governance

C) Earnings, Share Growth, and Gains

D) Efficiency, Stability, and Growth

17. A "hedge" in investment terms is:

A) A strategy used to limit or offset the probability of loss from fluctuations in the prices of commodities, currencies, or securities

B) A type of mutual fund

C) An investment in precious metals exclusively

D) A long-term stock holding strategy

18. What is the primary goal of portfolio rebalancing?

A) To ensure the portfolio maintains a set level of risk over time

B) To concentrate investments in a single asset class

C) To eliminate all risk from the portfolio

D) To switch to a completely different investment strategy annually

19. "Impact investing" focuses on:

A) Generating a financial return while also creating a positive social or environmental impact

B) Maximizing returns without regard for social or environmental consequences

C) Investing solely in government bonds

D) Short-term trading for quick profits

20. The strategy of "short selling" involves:

A) Borrowing shares of stock to sell at current market prices with the hope of buying them back later at a lower price

B) Purchasing undervalued stocks in bulk

C) Investing in short-term bonds exclusively

D) Selling assets that are expected to increase in value

21. Fundamental analysis in investment strategy focuses on:

A) Chart patterns and price movements

B) Economic indicators and market cycles

C) Evaluating a company's financial health and business prospects to determine its stock's intrinsic value

D) The timing of market entry and exit points

22. An investor focusing on "capital preservation" as their primary goal is most likely to invest in:

A) High-volatility stocks

B) Commodities trading

C) High-yield bonds

D) Treasury securities and money market funds

23. Which strategy involves investing in companies that pay high dividends?

A) Growth investing

B) Value investing

C) Income investing

D) Momentum investing

24. What is the primary focus of socially responsible investing (SRI)?

A) Maximizing returns regardless of the company's business activities

B) Investing only in companies that meet certain ethical, social, and environmental criteria

C) Focusing solely on financial metrics without considering the company's broader impact

D) Investing in companies with the highest dividend yields

25. An investor looking to protect against currency risk in international investments might use:

A) Currency hedging

B) Market timing

C) Sector rotation

D) Short selling

26. What does "leveraging" in investment strategy refer to?

A) Avoiding debt instruments

B) Using borrowed money to increase the potential return of an investment

C) Investing only in leveraged ETFs

D) Reducing investment in volatile markets

27. The strategy of rebalancing a portfolio involves:

A) Keeping the asset mix constant over time

B) Adjusting the proportions of different assets to maintain a desired asset allocation

C) Shifting all investments into cash at market highs

D) Investing more heavily in underperforming assets without regard to the original asset allocation

28. Which investment strategy aims to benefit from short-term market movements?

A) Buy and hold

B) Value investing

C) Day trading

D) Income investing

29. In the context of mutual funds, what is an "index fund"?

A) A fund that aims to outperform the market index

B) A fund that invests in companies across all sectors indiscriminately

C) A fund designed to replicate the performance of a specific market index

D) A fund that only invests in stocks not included in major market indices

30. What is the primary advantage of using a robo-advisor for investment management?

A) Guaranteed higher returns than any other investment strategy

B) Personal advice from a seasoned financial advisor

C) Lower costs and automated portfolio management based on algorithms

D) Exclusive access to high-risk, high-reward investments

31. "Arbitrage" involves:

A) Holding onto investments for long periods regardless of market conditions

B) Taking advantage of price differences in different markets or forms for the same asset

C) Investing in assets with guaranteed returns

D) Avoiding investments in the stock market

32. A "balanced fund" typically invests in:

A) Only blue-chip stocks

B) A mix of stocks, bonds, and sometimes cash equivalents to provide both income and growth

C) Real estate exclusively

D) Commodities like gold and silver

33. What is the goal of a "capital growth" investment strategy?

A) To ensure steady income from investments

B) To increase the value of the principal amount invested over time

C) To focus exclusively on investments that offer tax benefits

D) To invest in fixed-income securities only

34. "Strategic asset allocation" refers to:

A) A short-term investment approach that changes with market conditions

B) Setting long-term asset mix targets and periodically rebalancing back to those targets

C) Ignoring market trends and focusing on speculative investments

D) Allocating all assets into a single investment to maximize returns

35. The use of "options" in investment strategies can:

A) Only provide speculative opportunities with no real value

B) Serve as a way to hedge against potential losses or to speculate on market movements

C) Guarantee a fixed return on investment

D) Eliminate the risk of loss in a portfolio

36. "Value at risk" (VaR) is a tool used to:

A) Measure the maximum potential loss in an investment over a specific time period at a certain confidence level

B) Determine the exact return on investment for any given stock

C) Calculate the annual dividends paid by a company

D) Assess the ethical value of an investment

37. Investing in "emerging markets" is typically seen as:

A) A low-risk strategy suitable for conservative investors

B) A way to diversify a portfolio and potentially achieve higher returns, albeit with higher risk

C) Avoided by most seasoned investors due to the lack of opportunities

D) Equivalent to investing in developed markets in terms of risk and return

38. "Dividend reinvestment plans" (DRIPs) allow investors to:

A) Withdraw dividends in cash immediately

B) Automatically reinvest dividends to purchase additional shares of the stock

C) Invest dividends in unrelated companies

D) Convert dividends into bonds or other fixed-income securities

39. The concept of "compounding" in investing refers to:

A) The process of accumulating interest on an investment, where the amount of interest earned itself earns interest over time

B) Reducing investment risk by diversifying across different asset classes

C) The act of combining different types of investments into a single portfolio

D) The method of calculating interest rates on bonds

40. A "defensive investment strategy" is primarily focused on:

A) Maximizing returns by investing in high-growth stocks

B) Reducing potential losses during market downturns

C) Speculating on future market movements

D) Investing exclusively in government securities

41. "Smart beta" investing strategies aim to:

A) Follow a fixed index regardless of market conditions

B) Combine the benefits of passive and active investing to improve returns or reduce risk

C) Increase investment in technology startups

D) Focus solely on beta as a measure of investment worthiness

42. "Real estate investment trusts" (REITs) are popular among investors looking to:

A) Invest directly in physical properties without owning them

B) Avoid investing in the stock market

C) Focus exclusively on agricultural land investments

D) Invest in government securities only

43. The principle of "contractionary monetary policy" is to:

A) Encourage spending and investment by lowering interest rates

B) Reduce inflation and slow economic growth by increasing interest rates

C) Directly invest government funds into the stock market

D) Decrease the national debt by selling government assets

44. "Market capitalization" refers to:

A) The total value of all stocks traded on the stock market

B) The maximum amount a company can borrow from banks

C) The total value of a company's outstanding shares of stock

D) The capital allocated to the market by the government

MARKET DYNAMICS

1. What does the term "market liquidity" refer to?

A) The ability of a market to accept large transactions without impacting the price of the security

B) The total value of all securities within the market

C) The ease with which an asset can be converted into cash

D) Both A and C are correct

2. Market volatility is:

A) A measure of the price stability of securities within the market

B) The likelihood of rapid and significant price changes in a market

C) Only relevant to the stock market

D) Generally preferred by long-term investors

3. What is meant by "market depth"?

A) The extent to which a market can sustain large order sizes without affecting the price of the security

B) The variety of different securities available in a market

C) The level of expertise among traders in a particular market

D) The historical performance of a market over time

4. The "bid-ask spread" is:

A) The difference between the highest price a buyer is willing to pay and the lowest price a seller is willing to accept

B) A strategy used by traders to maximize profits

C) Irrelevant in modern electronic markets

D) Fixed for all securities

5. A "bull market" is characterized by:

A) Falling prices and pessimism among investors

B) Rising prices and optimism among investors

C) High liquidity and low volatility

D) Low trading volumes and high uncertainty

6. A "bear market" is characterized by:

A) Rising prices and optimism among investors

B) Falling prices and pessimism among investors

C) High volatility and high liquidity

D) Stagnant prices and low trading volumes

7. The "efficient market hypothesis" suggests that:

A) All known information is already reflected in stock prices

B) Only insider information can give an investor an advantage

C) Markets are rarely efficient

D) Stock prices are primarily driven by investor psychology

8. "High-frequency trading" (HFT) refers to:

A) Trading strategies that hold securities for long periods

B) The use of sophisticated algorithms to execute trades at very high speeds

C) A technique used only by retail investors

D) Trading based on fundamental analysis

9. What role do "market makers" play in the financial markets?

A) They ensure that markets remain inefficient

B) They provide liquidity by always being ready to buy or sell at publicly quoted prices

C) They predict market movements and inform investors

D) They regulate the markets to prevent fraud

10. "Short selling" involves:

A) Buying a stock with the expectation that it will increase in value

B) Borrowing a stock to sell it with the intention of buying it back later at a lower price

C) Selling a stock immediately after purchasing it

D) Investing in short-term government securities

11. The primary function of the "secondary market" is to:

A) Issue new securities

B) Allow investors to buy and sell securities among themselves

C) Provide loans to corporations and governments

D) Act as a regulatory body for the financial markets

12. "Price elasticity" in the context of market dynamics refers to:

A) The responsiveness of a security's price to changes in market interest rates

B) The stability of a market's pricing mechanisms over time

C) How sensitive the price of a security is to changes in supply and demand

D) The fixed pricing structure of commodities markets

13. A "circuit breaker" in financial markets is designed to:

A) Prevent traders from making too many transactions in a day

B) Temporarily halt trading to curb panic-selling on days of extreme volatility

C) Break the circuit of high-frequency trading algorithms

D) Permanently stop trading in a security that has lost all value

14. "Market sentiment" can be described as:

A) The underlying fundamentals of the economy

B) The overall attitude of investors toward a particular security or the market in general

C) A technical indicator used in stock analysis

D) The legal framework governing market operations

15. "Portfolio diversification" aims to:

A) Concentrate investments in a single sector to maximize returns

B) Reduce risk by spreading investments across various asset classes and sectors

C) Increase the liquidity of an investment portfolio

D) Focus solely on high-yield bonds

16. The "primary market" is where:

A) Securities are traded between investors without involving the issuing company

B) New securities are issued and sold for the first time

C) Only bonds are traded

D) Securities are retired from circulation

17. An "IPO" (Initial Public Offering) refers to:

A) The process by which a private company becomes publicly traded by offering its shares to the public for the first time

B) A company's decision to buy back its shares from the public

C) The annual meeting of a company's shareholders

D) The final trading day of a stock

18. "Market capitalization" is calculated by:

A) Multiplying the total number of a company's outstanding shares by the current market price of one share

B) Adding the total assets of a company

C) Subtracting a company's liabilities from its assets

D) The total volume of shares traded in a day

19. In financial markets, "liquidity risk" refers to:

A) The risk that an investor will not be able to buy a security

B) The risk associated with the inability to sell an investment at its current value

C) The risk of a market crash

D) The risk of interest rates rising

20. "Arbitrage" is best described as:

A) The practice of taking advantage of a price difference between two or more markets

B) A long-term investment strategy

C) The illegal practice of manipulating market prices

D) A form of high-frequency trading

21. The term "overbought" in market dynamics suggests that:

A) A security is undervalued and a good buy

B) A security has been sold too much and is due for a rebound

C) A security is considered too expensive relative to its true value and might be due for a downturn

D) The market as a whole is undervalued

22. "Market correction" refers to:

A) A rapid increase in market prices

B) A temporary reversal of a downward market trend

C) A short-term decline of 10% or more in the market or a security to adjust for overvaluation

D) Permanent changes in market regulation

23. What is the primary function of a stock exchange?

A) To regulate market volatility

B) To issue new securities

C) To facilitate the trading of securities

D) To provide loans to corporations

24. What does the term "market order" mean in trading?

A) An order to buy or sell a security at the current market price

B) An order to buy or sell a security in the future

C) An order to negotiate the price with the seller

D) An order to hold a security without trading it

25. When does "after-hours trading" occur?

A) Only during weekends

B) Before the regular market trading hours and after market close

C) Only on holidays

D) During regular market trading hours

26. What is a "limit order"?

A) An order that has no price limit

B) An order to buy or sell a security at a specific price or better

C) An order that is executed immediately at the current market price

D) An order that can only be placed during market holidays

27. What does the term "market capitalization" represent for a company?

A) The total assets of the company

B) The total liabilities of the company

C) The total value of all outstanding shares of the company's stock

D) The company's annual revenue

28. In market dynamics, what is "volume" referring to?

A) The loudness of trading floor noise

B) The total number of shares or contracts traded in a security or market during a given period

C) The weight of securities traded

D) The market capitalization of a company

29. What does the term "bid price" represent in a market?

A) The price at which a seller is willing to sell a security

B) The price at which a buyer is willing to buy a security

C) The last traded price of a security

D) The opening price of a security

30. What is the role of "market surveillance" in financial markets?

A) To ensure market prices remain fixed

B) To monitor trading activities for compliance with regulations and detect unusual trading patterns

C) To determine the market opening and closing times

D) To facilitate high-frequency trading

31. What is the primary purpose of a "stock index"?

A) To track the performance of a single company's stock

B) To measure the overall performance of a group of stocks

C) To regulate stock trading

D) To predict future stock prices

32. When a stock or market index is said to be "overvalued," what does it mean?

A) The stock or index is expected to decrease in value

B) The stock or index is expected to increase in value

C) The stock or index is trading at a price higher than its true value

D) The stock or index has no value

33. What is the "52-week high" and "52-week low" of a stock?

A) The highest and lowest prices a stock has traded at in the last 52 days

B) The highest and lowest prices a stock has traded at in the last 52 minutes

C) The highest and lowest prices a stock has traded at in the last 52 weeks

D) The highest and lowest prices a stock is projected to reach in the next 52 weeks

34. What does the term "stock split" mean?

A) The division of a company's stock into multiple classes

B) The combination of two different stocks into one

C) The process of issuing new shares to existing shareholders, increasing the number of shares outstanding

D) The process of delisting a stock from a stock exchange

35. In market dynamics, what is "market sentiment"?

A) The collective mood of investors regarding the stock market

B) The price of a stock at the moment of its initial public offering (IPO)

C) The official stance of the government regarding market regulation

D) The legal framework governing stock markets

36. What is the "closing price" of a security or index?

A) The price at which a security or index starts trading for the day

B) The price at which a security or index ends trading for the day

C) The highest price a security or index reaches during the day

D) The lowest price a security or index reaches during the day

37. How is the "market capitalization" of a company calculated?

A) By multiplying the total number of outstanding shares by the company's annual revenue

B) By multiplying the total number of outstanding shares by the current market price of one share

C) By subtracting the company's liabilities from its total assets

D) By dividing the company's total assets by its total liabilities

38. What is the "dividend yield" of a stock?

A) The annual interest rate paid by a company on its outstanding bonds

B) The annual income generated by a stock, expressed as a percentage of its current market price

C) The annual revenue of a company

D) The annual growth rate of a company's stock price

39. What is the role of "market makers" in stock trading?

A) To predict future stock prices

B) To regulate market volatility

C) To ensure that markets remain inefficient

D) To provide liquidity by always being ready to buy or sell at publicly quoted prices

40. What does "short covering" refer to in trading?

A) The process of buying a stock with the expectation that its price will rise

B) The process of selling a stock with the expectation that its price will fall

C) The process of buying back borrowed shares to close out a short position

D) The process of selling borrowed shares to open a short position

41. What is a "penny stock"?

A) A stock that costs only one cent per share

B) A stock with a market price below $5 per share and often characterized by high volatility

C) A stock issued by a government

D) A stock with a market price above $100 per share

42. In market dynamics, what does "diversification" aim to achieve for a portfolio?

A) To concentrate all investments in a single asset class

B) To increase risk by investing in highly correlated assets

C) To reduce risk by spreading investments across various asset classes and sectors

D) To maximize short-term gains regardless of long-term consequences

43. What does "market manipulation" involve?

A) Legal and ethical trading practices

B) Deliberate actions to artificially inflate or deflate market prices or trading volumes

C) Routine market analysis

D) The process of short selling

44. What does the term "volatility index" (VIX) measure?

A) The total trading volume of a stock

B) The level of market uncertainty and expected price fluctuations

C) The number of securities listed on a stock exchange

D) The average dividend yield of stocks in an index

21. ANSWERS AND EXPLANATIONS

A: Understanding Products and Their Risks

A: EQUITIES

1. B - Preferred stock typically has a higher claim on assets and earnings, which means they get dividends before common stockholders and have priority in the event of liquidation.

2. D - A stock split increases the number of shares outstanding, making the stock more accessible to a wider range of investors without affecting the company's market capitalization.

3. B - Blue-chip stocks are from large, well-established companies known for their financial stability, making them a safer investment during volatile market conditions.

4. B - Growth stocks are characterized by rapid growth in revenue and earnings, often reinvesting profits into the company rather than paying dividends.

5. C - Market capitalization is calculated by multiplying the current stock price by the total number of outstanding shares, representing the total value of the company in the market.

6. A - Liquidity refers to how easily stocks can be bought or sold in the market without significantly affecting the stock price, facilitating smoother transactions.

7. A - A bear market is defined by a decline in stock prices by 20% or more from recent highs, indicating widespread pessimism in the market.

8. B - The P/E ratio assesses a stock's share price relative to its earnings per share, helping investors determine if a stock is overvalued or undervalued.

9. A - Dividend yield is the ratio of a company's annual dividends compared to its share price, indicating how much investors earn from dividends relative to the stock price.

10. A - An Initial Public Offering (IPO) is when a company offers stocks to the public for the first time. This process allows a company to raise capital from public investors. The transition from a private to a public company can significantly increase a company's equity base and public awareness of the company. IPOs are often issued by smaller, younger companies seeking capital to expand, but can also be done by large privately-owned companies looking to become publicly traded.

11. C - Insider trading involves trading based on material, non-public information, which is illegal and unethical as it gives an unfair advantage over other investors who do not have access to this information.

12. B - A limit order allows an investor to specify a price at which they are willing to buy or sell a stock, ensuring that the trade is executed at that price or better.

13. B - Earnings per share (EPS) is a measure of a company's profitability, calculated as the portion of a company's profit allocated to each outstanding share of common stock, serving as an indicator of the company's financial health.

14. B - A stock's beta measures its volatility in comparison to the overall market. A beta greater than 1 indicates that the stock is more volatile than the market, while a beta less than 1 indicates it is less volatile.

15. B - A high P/E ratio might suggest that a stock is overvalued or that investors are expecting high growth rates in the future.

16. B - Short selling is a strategy used by investors who anticipate that a stock's price will decrease. They borrow shares to sell them at the current price, hoping to buy them back at a lower price.

17. B - The ex-dividend date is crucial because investors must own the stock before this date to be eligible for the next dividend payment.

18. B - A market order guarantees execution but not the price at which the trade will be executed, making it suitable for investors who prioritize completing the trade over securing a specific price.

19. B - A rights offering is an opportunity for existing shareholders to purchase additional shares at a discount before the new shares are offered to the public, allowing them to maintain their proportional ownership.

20. B - The book value of a stock is calculated from the company's balance sheet as total tangible assets minus total liabilities, offering a measure of the net asset value.

21. B - Penny stocks are known for their low prices and high volatility, often considered speculative investments due to their small market capitalization and limited liquidity.

22. B - Defensive stocks are expected to provide consistent dividends and stability even during economic downturns, making them attractive to investors looking for safer investment options during volatile periods.

23. B - Cyclical stocks are those whose performance is closely tied to the economic cycle, often performing well during economic expansions and poorly during recessions.

24. B - Stock exchanges facilitate the buying and selling of stocks, providing a platform for these transactions to occur.

25. B - A decrease in market interest rates often leads to an increase in stock prices as investors look for higher returns than what is offered by fixed-income securities.

26. B - A stock is considered "overvalued" when it is trading at a price that exceeds its fundamental value, which may be determined by factors like earnings, assets, and revenue.

27. B - Dividend reinvestment plans (DRIPs) allow investors to use dividends to purchase additional shares of the company's stock, often without a commission, facilitating the compounding of their investment.

28. C - A stop-loss order is designed to limit an investor's loss on a stock position by triggering a sell order at a certain price.

29. D - A high turnover rate in a portfolio leads to increased transaction costs and potential tax implications, which can erode investment returns.

30. B - Sector rotation refers to the movement of investments from one industry sector to another based on economic forecasts, as investors try to anticipate which sectors will perform well.

31. C - Treasury bonds are considered a safe investment, especially during stock market downturns, as they are backed by the U.S. government.

32. C - The "bid" price is the lowest price a buyer is willing to pay for a stock, reflecting the demand side of the market equation.

33. A - The "float" refers to the total number of shares available for trading by the public, excluding shares held by insiders and major shareholders.

34. D - Penny stocks carry a high risk of loss due to their low prices, high volatility, and often limited liquidity.

35. A - The "ask" price is the price a seller is willing to accept for the stock, representing the supply side of the market equation.

36. B - A "growth" investment strategy focuses on stocks of companies expected to grow at an above-average rate compared to their industry, aiming for capital appreciation.

37. A - The "ex-dividend" date is the date by which investors must hold the stock to be eligible to receive the next dividend payment, after which the stock trades without the dividend value.

38. C - A large-cap fund specifically invests in companies with large market capitalizations, aiming to provide stable returns from well-established companies.

39. B - The "volume" of a stock traded refers to the number of shares that were bought and sold during a specific period, indicating the stock's liquidity and investor interest.

40. B - An "index fund" aims to replicate the performance of a specific market index, providing investors with a diversified portfolio that mirrors the overall market performance.

41. A - A "margin call" occurs when the equity in a margin account falls below a certain level, prompting the broker to request additional funds or securities to maintain the required margin.

42. B - "Market depth" refers to the extent to which a market can absorb large orders without significantly impacting the price of a security, indicating liquidity and the ability to execute large trades.

43. B - A "market order" is executed at the best available price at the time of the order, ensuring execution but not a specific price.

44. B - The "return on equity" (ROE) measures a company's ability to generate profits from its shareholders' equity, indicating how efficiently the company uses its capital to generate earnings.

A: PACKAGED PRODUCTS

1. B - Mutual funds pool money from many investors to invest in a diversified portfolio of stocks, bonds, or other securities, offering diversification and professional management.

2. B - ETFs offer the diversification of a mutual fund but are traded on exchanges like stocks, allowing for intraday trading.

3. B - The primary advantage of investing in a mutual fund is accessing professional management, helping investors who may not have the time or expertise to manage their investments.

4. B - ETFs are most likely to track an index, providing a cost-effective way for investors to gain exposure to a broad market or specific sector.

5. B - REITs invest in real estate and real estate-related assets, offering investors a way to gain exposure to real estate without directly owning property.

6. B - Closed-end funds have a fixed number of shares and are traded on stock exchanges like stocks, differing from open-end funds, which do not have a fixed number of shares and are not traded on exchanges.

7. B - Hedge funds are private investment partnerships open to a limited number of accredited investors and require significant initial minimum investments, known for their aggressive investment strategies.

8. B - UITs offer a fixed portfolio of securities with a definite termination date, unlike mutual funds, which have a constantly changing portfolio.

9. B - Money market funds aim to maintain a stable share price and offer liquidity, investing in short-term, high-quality debt securities.

10. B - Municipal bond funds invest in tax-exempt municipal bonds, offering investors tax-exempt income, making them attractive to investors in higher tax brackets.

11. C - Target-date funds are designed for investors saving for a specific goal with a known time horizon, such as retirement, automatically adjusting the asset mix as the target date approaches.

12. C - The expense ratio represents the annual fee that all funds charge their shareholders, expressed as a percentage of the fund's average assets under management.

13. B - ETFs are considered the most liquid among the options because they trade on stock exchanges like individual stocks, allowing for easy buying and selling.

14. B - Sector funds invest in a specific sector of the economy, offering potential for high returns but also higher risk due to lack of diversification.

15. A - The NAV of a mutual fund is the total value of the fund's holdings minus its liabilities, divided by the number of shares outstanding, representing the per-share value of the fund.

16. B - Balanced funds provide a mix of growth, income, and stability by investing in a diversified portfolio of stocks, bonds, and other securities, suitable for investors seeking a moderate risk profile.

17. C - An advantage of investing in an index fund is the lower expense ratios compared to actively managed funds, due to the passive management strategy of simply tracking an index.

18. A - A commodity fund invests in physical commodities or commodity-linked derivative instruments, including precious metals like gold and silver.

19. C - Not all ETFs track an index; some are actively managed. While many ETFs are designed to track the performance of a specific index, there are also actively managed ETFs that do not follow an index.

20. B - International funds invest in securities from markets outside the investor's country of residence, offering diversification and exposure to foreign markets.

21. D - The primary risk of investing in a sector fund is the lack of diversification, as investing heavily in one sector can lead to higher volatility and risk if that sector underperforms.

22. C - Dividend income funds focus on investing in companies that pay regular, high dividends, appealing to investors seeking regular income from their investments.

23. B - Money market funds are designed for capital preservation and liquidity, making them suitable for investors seeking to minimize risk.

24. C - ETFs are unique for their ability to be traded intraday like stocks, offering flexibility not found in mutual funds.

25. B - Balanced funds aim to allocate investments across various asset classes, such as stocks and bonds, to balance risk and return.

26. B - The primary goal of an income fund is to generate regular income for its investors through dividends or interest payments.

27. B - Utility funds primarily invest in utility companies and aim to provide returns through dividends, focusing on capital protection.

28. A - Investing in international funds carries currency risk, among other risks, due to investments across different countries.

29. B - No-load funds do not charge any fees for buying or selling shares, distinguishing them from load funds, which do.

30. B - Money market funds invest in short-term, high-quality debt securities, offering investors liquidity and a higher degree of safety.

31. B - An index fund that tracks the S&P 500 is designed to mirror the performance of the S&P 500, providing broad market exposure.

32. B - Hedge funds are known for using strategies like leverage, short-selling, and derivatives to amplify returns and manage risk.

33. B - Actively managed funds have fund managers making investment decisions, aiming to outperform the market or achieve specific investment objectives.

34. B - A "fund of funds" invests in other mutual funds or ETFs, offering diversification by pooling investments across various funds.

35. B - Target-date funds automatically adjust their asset allocation, becoming more conservative as the target date (e.g., retirement) approaches.

36. B - Municipal bond funds offer tax advantages, as the interest income from municipal bonds is often exempt from federal income tax and sometimes state and local taxes.

37. C - Inverse ETFs aim to deliver the opposite of the performance of their benchmark index, offering a way to profit from or hedge against declines in the market.

38. B - High yield bond funds invest in bonds rated below investment grade, offering higher returns but with higher risk due to the increased likelihood of default.

39. B - Socially responsible funds allow investors to invest in companies that meet certain ethical, social, and environmental criteria, aligning investment choices with personal values.

40. B - REITs can provide a hedge against inflation as real estate values and rents typically increase when inflation rises, potentially leading to higher returns.

41. C - Asset allocation funds maintain a fixed allocation of assets among different categories like stocks, bonds, and cash, adjusting the mix according to the fund's investment strategy.

42. A - Leveraged ETFs seek to deliver multiples of the daily performance of the index they track, using financial derivatives and debt to amplify returns.

43. B - Venture capital funds provide capital to start-up companies with high growth potential, taking on higher risk for the possibility of high returns.

44. B - Global funds invest in both U.S. and non-U.S. markets, offering broader diversification compared to international funds, which invest only in non-U.S. markets.

A: OPTIONS

1. B - Buying a call option gives the holder the right to buy a stock at a predetermined price, typically with the expectation that the stock price will rise.

2. A - Selling a put option indicates the seller expects the market to rise, as they are obligated to buy the stock at the strike price if the buyer exercises the option.

3. C - A covered call strategy involves selling a call option while owning the equivalent amount of the underlying stock, aiming to generate income from the option premium.

4. A - The strike price is the price at which the holder of an option can exercise the option to buy (call) or sell (put) the underlying stock.

5. C - A long straddle benefits from an increase in volatility, as it involves buying both a call and a put option, profiting from significant moves in either direction.

6. B - A call option is 'in the money' when the strike price is below the market price of the underlying asset, making it profitable to exercise.

7. B - The maximum loss for the buyer of a put option is limited to the premium paid for the option, regardless of how much the underlying stock price moves.

8. B - Writing a naked put exposes the seller to the risk of the stock's price falling below the strike price, as they may have to buy the stock at the strike price.

9. B - American-style options can be exercised at any time before expiration, offering more flexibility than European-style options, which can only be exercised at expiration.

10. B - An option's premium is the price paid by the buyer to the seller to acquire the rights that the option confers.

11. A - The breakeven point for a call option buyer is the strike price plus the premium paid, as this is the price at which the option starts to be profitable.

12. B - A straddle involves buying both a call and a put option on the same stock with the same expiration and strike price, betting on volatility without predicting direction.

13. B - The intrinsic value of a put option increases as the underlying stock's price decreases, making the option more valuable.

14. A - The expiration date is the last date on which the option can be exercised, after which it becomes worthless.

15. C - A protective put strategy involves buying a put option to protect against a decline in the value of stock that is owned, acting as insurance.

16. C - If an option expires 'out of the money,' it means the option cannot be exercised profitably and thus expires worthless.

17. C - The delta of an option measures the sensitivity of the option's price to a one-point move in the underlying asset, indicating how much the price of the option is expected to change.

18. B - Selling a naked call is considered the most risky because if the stock price rises significantly, the seller faces unlimited potential losses.

19. A - The 'time value' of an option is the portion of the option's premium that exceeds its intrinsic value, reflecting the potential for the option to become profitable prior to expiration.

20. C - A call option is 'at the money' when the strike price and the current market price of the underlying stock are equal.

21. C - A long straddle strategy is used when an investor expects a stock's price to move significantly but is unsure of the direction, buying both a call and a put option.

22. B - The implied volatility of an option reflects the market's view of the expected volatility of the stock price until the option's expiration, influencing the option's premium.

23. B - When selling a covered call option, the stock may be called away (sold) if the stock price exceeds the strike price, limiting the seller's profit potential to the premium received plus any gain up to the strike price.

24. C - Theta represents the rate at which an option's price decays over time, reflecting the time value component of the option's premium.

25. B - A put option is considered 'deep in the money' when the strike price is significantly higher than the current market price of the stock, increasing the option's intrinsic value.

26. C - A synthetic long stock strategy involves selling a put option and buying a call option with the same expiration date and strike price, mimicking the payoff of owning the actual stock.

27. B - Options are used in portfolios primarily to hedge against potential losses, providing insurance against adverse price movements in the underlying assets.

28. C - This strategy, known as a synthetic long stock, involves buying a call option and selling a put option with the same strike price and expiration, simulating the economic effect of owning the stock.

29. A - Gamma measures the rate of change of the option's delta, indicating how the delta will change as the underlying stock price moves, which is crucial for understanding the option's price sensitivity.

30. A - Selling a naked call option has limited profit potential (the premium received) and unlimited loss potential, as the seller is obligated to deliver the stock at the strike price if the option is exercised, regardless of how high the stock's price may rise.

31. B - Vega indicates how the option's price changes with a 1% change in the implied volatility of the underlying asset, highlighting the sensitivity of the option's price to changes in market volatility.

32. D - A collar strategy involves owning the underlying stock, buying a put option to protect against downside risk, and selling a call option to offset the cost of the put, effectively hedging the stock's position.

33. C - An 'at the money' put option has a strike price equal to the current market price of the underlying stock, making it neither profitable nor unprofitable at the moment.

34. A - The intrinsic value of a call option is the current stock price minus the strike price, if positive; otherwise, it is zero, representing the profit that could be made if the option were exercised immediately.

35. B - A long put strategy allows an investor to profit from a decrease in a stock's price without owning the stock, providing a right to sell the stock at the strike price.

36. B - The maximum profit for a long put option holder is limited to the strike price minus the premium paid if the stock goes to zero, as the option gives the right to sell the stock at the strike price.

37. C - Buying a call option is suited for an investor expecting a moderate increase in the underlying stock's price, offering unlimited profit potential with limited loss (the premium paid).

38. B - The break-even point for a put option seller is the strike price minus the premium received, representing the price at which the seller neither makes nor loses money.

39. C - An option with no intrinsic value (the stock price is not favorable compared to the strike price) and only time value is said to be 'out of the money.'

40. A - A risk reversal strategy involves buying a call and selling a put with the same expiration and strike price, aiming to mimic the payoff of a long stock position while using options.

41. D - A bear spread is used to hedge against or profit from a decline in the underlying asset's price, with limited loss and profit potential structured through the use of put or call options.

42. A - The leverage effect of options allows investors to control a large amount of the underlying asset with a relatively small investment, amplifying both potential gains and losses.

43. B - Rho measures the sensitivity of the option's price to changes in interest rates, indicating how the price of the option is expected to change as interest rates move.

44. B - A butterfly spread involves buying two call options at different strike prices and selling one call option at a middle strike price, aiming to profit from low volatility in the underlying asset.

A: Understanding Trading, Customer Accounts, and Prohibited Activities

TYPES OF ORDERS

1. B - The primary purpose of a market order is to execute a trade immediately at the best available price, prioritizing speed over price control.

2. B - A limit order allows a trader to specify the maximum or minimum price at which they are willing to buy or sell, providing control over the execution price.

3. C - A stop-loss order is designed to sell a stock when it falls to a certain price, helping to limit an investor's loss on a position.

4. B - A stop order becomes a market order once the stop price is reached, aiming to execute as soon as possible at the current market price.

5. A - A stop-limit order executes at a specified price or better after a given stop price has been reached, combining the features of stop and limit orders.

6. C - A stop-loss order can help protect profits on a stock by setting a sell price below the current market price to limit potential losses.

7. B - The main difference between a stop order and a stop-limit order is that a stop order becomes a market order when triggered, while a stop-limit order becomes a limit order.

8. B - If an investor places a limit order to sell a stock at $50 and the stock's price jumps to $55, the order may be executed at $55 or a better price, not just at $50.

9. B - A limit order is used by an investor who wants to enter a position at a specific price or better, ensuring price control.

10. C - To sell a stock as it falls to limit losses, an investor should use a stop-loss order, which triggers a sale when the stock reaches a certain downward price.

11. A - The risk of placing a stop-loss order is that the stock may rebound after the order is executed, potentially resulting in missed gains.

12. B - A GTC (Good Till Canceled) order remains active until it is executed or canceled by the trader, providing flexibility in order duration.

13. B - In a rapidly rising market, a market order is likely to result in the highest execution price for a sell order due to immediate execution at current prices.

14. A - An all-or-none (AON) order must be executed in its entirety or not at all, ensuring that partial fills do not occur.

15. B - The primary advantage of using a limit order over a market order is the ability to specify a price, offering control over the execution price.

16. B - In volatile markets, a stop-limit order may not execute if the stock price moves past the limit price too quickly, presenting a risk of non-execution.

17. B - If the limit price of a stop-limit order is not reached, the order remains active until the limit price is reached or the order is canceled, without automatic conversion to a market order.

18. B - A day order expires if not executed by the close of the trading day it was placed, limiting its duration to a single trading session.

19. B - A limit order to buy is best used when an investor wants to purchase a stock only if it drops to a certain price or lower, offering price control.

20. A - The execution of a stop order depends on the stock reaching a specific price, which triggers the conversion to a market or limit order.

21. A - Fill or kill (FOK) orders require that the order be executed immediately in its entirety or not at all, ensuring immediate and complete execution or cancellation.

22. C - Market orders ensure execution but not a specific price, making them suitable for investors who prioritize completing a trade over obtaining a specific price.

23. A - The primary advantage of a trailing stop order is that it locks in profits while potentially allowing for further gains by adjusting the stop price as the market price moves in a favorable direction.

24. B - A discretionary order allows the broker discretion over the execution timing and price, aiming to achieve the best possible outcome for the client.

25. A - If a limit order to buy is placed above the current market price, it may be executed immediately, as the order price is already above the market price, indicating the buyer's willingness to pay more.

26. A - In a fast-moving market, the risk associated with a market order is slippage, where the order may be executed at a very different price from the current price due to rapid price changes.

27. A - A buy stop order is typically used to limit a loss on a short sale by buying the stock back if its price rises to a certain level, preventing further losses.

28. B - A bracket order sets a stop loss and take profit level at the same time, aiming to automatically close the position either at a predetermined profit level or to stop a loss.

29. B - A market-if-touched (MIT) order is similar to a limit order but is executed only if the market price touches the order price, aiming to buy or sell at a specific price if the market reaches that level.

30. B - The primary use of a stop order in a long position is to protect against a significant drop in the stock's price by setting a sell trigger if the price falls too much.

31. B - A sell stop-limit order becomes a limit order to sell when the stock falls to the stop price, specifying the minimum price at which the stock should be sold.

32. A - A 'not held' order gives the broker discretion over the execution timing and price, allowing for flexibility in seeking the best possible execution.

33. B - A market-on-close (MOC) order is an order to buy or sell a stock at the closing price of the market, aiming for execution at the end of the trading day.

34. A - The main purpose of an iceberg order is to hide the true size of an order by only revealing a small portion of it at a time, minimizing market impact.

35. B - A pegged order is adjusted based on changes in a benchmark rate or index, maintaining a relative value to the specified benchmark.

36. B - A day trader would most likely use a market order to quickly enter or exit a position to capitalize on short-term market movements, prioritizing speed over price.

37. A - A limit order book is used by traders to view all active limit orders for a particular stock, providing insight into potential support and resistance levels.

38. A - The primary risk of using a good-till-canceled (GTC) order is that the order may be forgotten and executed at an undesirable time if market conditions change.

39. B - A fill-or-kill (FOK) order is most appropriate when an investor requires immediate and complete execution of a large order, ensuring that the order is either fully executed right away or not at all.

40. B - The time-in-force condition on an order determines the duration for which the order is active, specifying how long the order should remain in the market before it is canceled.

41. B - The main advantage of using a volume-weighted average price (VWAP) order is that it helps in buying or selling a stock at a price close to the average price of the day, aiming for a fair execution price.

42. B - The execution of a hidden (or iceberg) order shows only a part of the order size to the market, aiming to minimize the market impact of large orders.

43. C - A sweep-to-fill order is designed to sweep through multiple price levels to fill the order as quickly as possible, capturing liquidity across different price points.

44. A - The use of a conditional order allows an investor to set conditions under which the order will automatically be executed or canceled, providing control over the execution based on specific market conditions.

ACCOUNT TYPES
----

1. B - A cash account requires investors to pay for securities in full at the time of purchase, unlike a margin account which allows borrowing to purchase securities.

2. B - A margin account is required for short selling because it involves borrowing shares to sell them in anticipation of buying them back at a lower price.

3. B - Roth IRAs offer tax-free withdrawals in retirement, providing a tax advantage over traditional IRAs, where contributions are tax-deductible but withdrawals are taxed.

4. B - In a JTWROS account, the surviving account holders automatically gain control of the account's assets upon the death of one party, facilitating the transfer of assets without the need for probate.

5. B - A UGMA account is managed by a custodian until the minor reaches a certain age, typically used for gifting assets to minors with some tax advantages.

6. D - A Coverdell Education Savings Account (ESA) is specifically designed for saving for education expenses, offering tax-free growth and withdrawals for qualified expenses.

7. B - A trust account is used to manage assets for the benefit of a third party, such as a beneficiary, with a trustee overseeing the account according to the trust's terms.

8. A - A discretionary account gives the broker the authority to make trades without the client's specific approval for each transaction, based on an agreed-upon strategy.

9. A - A TOD designation allows for the direct transfer of assets to a designated beneficiary upon the account holder's death, bypassing probate court.

10. C - A corporate investment account is opened in the name of a corporation for the purpose of investing corporate funds, distinct from individual or joint investment accounts.

11. B - An IRA offers tax advantages, such as tax-deferred growth or tax-free withdrawals, depending on the type of IRA (Traditional or Roth).

12. B - Prime brokerage accounts offer a range of services to large investors and institutions, including lending, cash management, and consolidated reporting, among others.

13. A - UTMA accounts allow for a wider range of assets to be gifted to minors compared to UGMA accounts, including real estate and patents, among others.

14. C - The main advantage of tax-deferred retirement accounts is the tax-free growth of investments until withdrawal, allowing investments to grow without being diminished by taxes annually.

15. A - A Coverdell ESA allows for tax-free withdrawals for qualified education expenses, offering a tax advantage for saving for education costs.

16. C - A global trading account is designed for investors looking to trade securities on international stock exchanges, offering access to foreign markets directly.

17. B - HSAs offer tax advantages for saving and paying for healthcare expenses, allowing contributions to be made with pre-tax dollars and withdrawals for qualified medical expenses to be tax-free.

18. B - Accredited investor accounts are for individuals who meet certain income or net worth criteria, providing access to investment opportunities not available to the general public, such as private placements.

19. B - Sweep accounts automatically invest excess cash balances into a money market fund or similar vehicle to earn short-term gains, optimizing the return on uninvested cash.

20. B - A Solo 401(k) plan is designed for self-employed individuals with no employees other than a spouse, offering a way to save for retirement with higher contribution limits compared to traditional IRAs.

21. A - Money purchase pension plans require employers to make fixed, annual contributions to their employees' retirement accounts, providing a predictable benefit structure.

22. B - Limited trading authorization grants a designated individual the ability to make trades on behalf of the account holder within specified limits, allowing for managed trading without full account control.

23. B - Managed accounts are designed for high-net-worth individuals, offering personalized investment strategies and services tailored to the individual's financial goals and risk tolerance.

24. A - A sweep account automatically moves cash balances into a higher interest-earning money market fund at the end of each day, optimizing the return on uninvested cash.

25. C - Dark pool accounts allow investors to execute large volume trades anonymously, minimizing market impact by not showing the order book to the public.

26. B - A custodial account allows adults to gift securities to minors, offering a tax-efficient way to transfer wealth while the assets are managed by a custodian until the minor reaches adulthood.

27. A - A mutual fund wrap account provides investors with a diversified portfolio of mutual funds selected based on the investor's risk tolerance and investment objectives, often for a single consolidated fee.

28. B - A cash management account consolidates banking and brokerage services, offering features like check writing and debit cards, simplifying financial management for investors.

29. C - Investment club accounts allow groups of investors to pool their resources to meet minimum investment requirements and invest collectively in securities.

30. A - A nominee account holds securities in the financial institution's name on behalf of the investor, simplifying the management and administration of investments.

31. C - A securities-based loan account allows investors to borrow against the value of their securities for purposes other than purchasing more securities, offering flexibility for personal or business financing needs.

32. D - A balanced fund account invests in a diversified portfolio of stocks and bonds as a single investment, aiming to provide a balance between growth and income.

33. C - A numbered account offers investors the ability to trade securities anonymously, protecting the identity of the investor in transactions.

34. C - A discretionary managed account is managed without the day-to-day involvement of the investor, with investment decisions made by a designated financial advisor or portfolio manager.

35. B - A Health Savings Account (HSA) is designed for saving for healthcare expenses with pre-tax dollars, offering tax advantages for contributions, growth, and qualified withdrawals.

36. A - A futures account allows for the trading of futures contracts and options on futures, catering to investors interested in commodities, currencies, and financial futures markets.

37. D - An accredited investor account may be required to participate in certain IPOs, especially those offering shares to investors meeting specific income or net worth criteria before public listing.

38. B - A Roth IRA is designed for saving for retirement with after-tax contributions, offering tax-free growth and tax-free withdrawals in retirement.

39. A - An employee stock purchase plan (ESPP) allows employees to purchase company stock at a discount, providing an incentive and benefit for employees to invest in their company.

40. C - A defined contribution plan allows for pre-tax contributions by the employer on behalf of the employee, with the retirement benefit based on the contributions and investment performance.

41. A - A dividend reinvestment plan (DRIP) allows investors to automatically reinvest dividends from stocks or mutual funds into additional shares, facilitating compound growth.

42. D - A direct market access (DMA) account is suitable for executing trades based on algorithmic trading strategies, offering sophisticated investors direct access to the markets for fast execution.

43. B - A 529 college savings plan is designed for saving for post-secondary education expenses, offering tax advantages and high contribution limits for education savings.

44. A - A securities lending account offers investors the opportunity to lend their securities to others for a lending fee, often used by other investors for short selling purposes.

PROHIBITED PRACTICES

1. B - Churning is a prohibited practice involving excessive trading in a client's account primarily to generate commissions.

2. B - Churning refers to excessive trading by a broker in a client's account to generate commissions, which is unethical and illegal.

3. A - Front-running is the unethical practice of executing orders on behalf of the firm before executing orders previously submitted by clients.

4. C - Pump and dump is a manipulative trading practice where prices are artificially inflated to sell off owned securities at a higher price.

5. A - Painting the tape involves creating a misleading appearance of active trading in a security to attract investors, which is manipulative and illegal.

6. B - Insider trading involves the use of non-public, material information to make investment decisions, which is illegal and unethical.

7. A - A wash sale involves selling a security at a loss and purchasing a substantially identical security within 30 days before or after the sale, which is prohibited to prevent tax deduction abuse.

8. A - Marking the close refers to the practice of placing trades at the end of the trading day to affect the closing price of a stock, which is manipulative.

9. A - Naked short selling is the illegal practice of selling a security without owning it or ensuring its availability for delivery.

10. B - Spoofing involves submitting large orders to create the illusion of interest in a stock, then canceling them, which is considered market manipulation.

11. A - Layering involves placing and then canceling orders to mislead other traders about the demand or supply of a security, which is a form of market manipulation.

12. B - Misrepresentation involves using misleading or false statements to sell investments, which is illegal and unethical.

13. A - Unauthorized trading occurs when a broker executes trades in a client's account without the client's specific approval, violating client trust.

14. A - Recommending securities without a reasonable basis is known as a suitability violation, which breaches the duty to act in the client's best interest.

15. C - Failing to disclose conflicts of interest to clients is a violation of ethical standards, as it prevents clients from making informed decisions.

16. C - Guaranteeing against loss to a client in a securities transaction is prohibited, as it misrepresents the risk inherent in securities trading.

17. B - Tying, or requiring a client to purchase one product to obtain another, is illegal or unethical as it restricts client choice and may not serve the client's best interest.

18. B - Scalping refers to brokers using their own accounts to acquire shares of a new issue before offering it to clients, which is considered unethical.

19. A - Laddering in securities issuance involves submitting fake bids to create the impression of high demand, which is illegal.

20. B - Naked short selling involves selling securities that one has not confirmed can be borrowed for delivery, which is prohibited in many jurisdictions.

21. A - Block trading consolidates orders from different clients into one block to execute a single trade, often used to manage large orders efficiently.

22. B - Free-riding involves selling securities bought with unsettled funds without covering the initial purchase, which violates the settlement rules.

23. B - Quote stuffing involves placing a large number of orders and then canceling them to slow down competitors, which disrupts the market's fairness and efficiency.

24. A - Momentum ignition refers to starting a trend by executing a series of transactions to create the appearance of rapid market movement, aiming to manipulate prices.

25. B - Blue sheeting refers to a request by regulatory authorities for detailed trades information to investigate suspicious trading activity or market manipulation.

26. A - Back running involves trading ahead of a client's transaction to benefit from the anticipated market impact, exploiting confidential client information.

27. A - Interpositioning occurs when a broker unnecessarily inserts an intermediary in a transaction to generate additional fees, increasing costs for the client without providing any benefit.

28. B - Pooling is considered prohibited when it involves creating a secret agreement among traders to manipulate stock prices, distorting the market's natural supply and demand.

29. B - Benchmark manipulation involves manipulating financial benchmarks or indices to benefit derivative positions, undermining the integrity of financial markets.

30. A - Cross trading is prohibited when it involves the buying and selling of securities between clients without actual change in ownership, potentially harming client interests.

31. B - Circular trading involves a group of traders buying and selling securities among themselves to create artificial trading volume, misleading other market participants.

32. B - Banging the close involves executing a flurry of trades just before the market close to influence the closing price, manipulating market prices in a deceptive manner.

33. A - Pre-arranged trading usually refers to setting up trades between parties at predetermined prices, which may not reflect the current market price, undermining market fairness.

34. B - Spoofing is designed to influence the price of a security by placing orders with no intention of executing them, creating a false impression of market interest.

35. B - Layering involves submitting and canceling orders to mislead participants about market demand, considered a manipulative and deceptive trading practice.

36. A - The use of material non-public information for trading purposes is prohibited because it constitutes insider trading, giving an unfair advantage over other market participants.

37. B - Matched orders create a false appearance of trading activity without actual change in ownership, considered manipulative as they mislead other market participants about the security's demand.

38. B - Flipping IPO shares refers to buying shares at the IPO price and selling them quickly after trading begins to profit from price jumps, which can be frowned upon by issuers.

39. B - Cornering the market involves acquiring sufficient shares of a particular security to control its price, which can be illegal and disrupts market integrity.

40. B - Rumormongering involves spreading unverified or false information to influence security prices, a manipulative practice that can lead to significant market distortions.

41. A - "Straw man" transactions refer to using a third party to conceal the true party in interest in a transaction, often to circumvent regulations or hide conflicts of interest.

42. B - Window dressing by investment managers involves making cosmetic changes to a portfolio before reporting periods to improve its appearance, potentially misleading investors.

43. A - Piggybacking in trading refers to following the trades of successful investors without independent analysis, which can lead to uninformed and risky investment decisions.

44. A - The unethical practice of libel in the securities market involves publishing false statements about a company to manipulate its stock price, damaging the company's reputation and investor trust.

A: Overview of the Regulatory Framework

REGULATORY AGENCY

1. B - The Securities and Exchange Commission (SEC) is the primary regulator of the U.S. securities markets, overseeing the enforcement of federal securities laws.

2. B - The Financial Industry Regulatory Authority (FINRA) oversees broker-dealers and registered representatives, ensuring they operate fairly and honestly.

3. B - The Securities Investor Protection Corporation (SIPC) protects investors from broker-dealer bankruptcy, insuring customers' cash and securities.

4. B - The Commodity Futures Trading Commission (CFTC) regulates futures and options markets, ensuring the integrity of commodities and financial futures markets.

5. C - The Securities and Exchange Commission (SEC) is responsible for enforcing federal securities laws, protecting investors and maintaining fair, orderly, and efficient markets.

6. B - The National Association of Securities Dealers (NASD) merged with NYSE Regulation to form the Financial Industry Regulatory Authority (FINRA), which is responsible for regulatory oversight of all securities firms that do business with the public.

7. C - State securities regulators are primarily responsible for enforcing state securities laws and regulations, licensing broker-dealers, and providing investor education.

8. B - The Office of the Comptroller of the Currency (OCC) regulates federal savings associations and national banks, ensuring the safety and soundness of the national banking system.

9. B - The Municipal Securities Rulemaking Board (MSRB) regulates the trading of municipal securities, setting rules to protect investors and the public interest.

10. B - The Securities and Exchange Commission (SEC) and state regulators are responsible for regulating investment advisers, overseeing their practices and disclosures to clients.

11. D - The primary function of the Public Company Accounting Oversight Board (PCAOB) is to oversee the audits of public companies and regulate public accounting firms to protect investors.

12. B - The Federal Deposit Insurance Corporation (FDIC) insures deposits in banks and thrift institutions, protecting depositors from bank failures.

13. D - The Securities and Exchange Commission (SEC) was established as a result of the Securities Exchange Act of 1934, following the stock market crash of 1929 to restore investor confidence.

14. A - The Consumer Financial Protection Bureau (CFPB) protects consumers from unfair, deceptive, or abusive practices in financial services, including banking, lending, and financial advisory services.

15. A - The Financial Crimes Enforcement Network (FinCEN) is a bureau of the U.S. Department of the Treasury, focused on combating money laundering, terrorist financing, and other financial crimes.

16. A - The North American Securities Administrators Association (NASAA) consists of securities regulators from the 50 states, the District of Columbia, Puerto Rico, and the U.S. territories, coordinating and advocating for investor protection.

17. B - The primary purpose of the Federal Reserve in the context of securities regulation is to oversee monetary policy and regulate banks, indirectly affecting the securities markets through its policies.

18. B - The Securities and Exchange Commission (SEC) enforces the Jumpstart Our Business Startups (JOBS) Act, which aims to make it easier for small businesses to raise funds and go public.

19. B - The National Futures Association (NFA) oversees futures markets, regulating firms and individuals who conduct futures trading, to protect investors and maintain market integrity.

20. B - The Investment Company Act of 1940 regulates mutual funds and other investment companies, setting standards for the industry to protect investors.

21. A - The Financial Stability Oversight Council (FSOC) was created to identify risks to the financial stability of the United States, coordinating across federal financial regulators.

22. A - The International Organization of Securities Commissions (IOSCO) focuses on coordinating global securities regulation, promoting high standards of regulation to ensure investor protection and market integrity.

23. B - FINRA's Code of Conduct sets forth the professional conduct standards for broker-dealers and registered representatives, ensuring ethical behavior in the securities industry.

24. C - Failure to adhere to "Know Your Customer" (KYC) rules can result in disciplinary actions by FINRA or the SEC, as it's crucial for preventing fraud and ensuring suitable recommendations.

25. B - FINRA Rule 2010 requires broker-dealers to uphold a high standard of commercial honor and just and equitable principles of trade, promoting integrity in the securities industry.

26. A - Suitability obligations require that a broker-dealer only recommend investments that are suitable for the client based on their financial situation and risk tolerance, ensuring clients' interests are protected.

27. D - Churning violates both Rule 2111 (Suitability) and Rule 2010 (Standards of Commercial Honor and Principles of Trade) as it involves unethical and excessive trading in a client's account.

28. A - The "Net Capital Rule" ensures that broker-dealers maintain sufficient liquidity to meet obligations to clients, protecting clients' assets and maintaining market integrity.

29. B - Anti-Money Laundering (AML) rules require broker-dealers to report suspicious transactions exceeding $5,000 to FinCEN, part of efforts to combat money laundering and financial crimes.

30. A - Regulation Best Interest (Reg BI) mandates that broker-dealers act in the best interest of their retail customers when making a recommendation, elevating the standard of care from the previous suitability standard.

31. B - The Office of Compliance Inspections and Examinations (OCIE) conducts examinations of SEC-regulated entities to ensure compliance with laws and regulations, aiming to protect investors and maintain market integrity.

32. A - The "Gift Rule" limits the value of gifts given by members to $100 per person per year, preventing potential conflicts of interest and ensuring fair business practices.

33. A - The "Taping Rule" requires certain broker-dealers to record all telephone conversations with clients, aimed at enhancing transparency and compliance with regulatory requirements.

34. A - Regulation Fair Disclosure (Reg FD) aims at preventing insider trading by requiring the fair disclosure of material information to all investors simultaneously, ensuring a level playing field.

35. B - The Consolidated Audit Trail (CAT) initiative requires broker-dealers to report certain transactions and order events to a central repository, enhancing market surveillance and regulatory oversight.

36. B - Under FINRA Rule 4512, member firms must make a reasonable effort to obtain information about the investment experience, financial status, and age of their clients, ensuring suitability of recommendations.

37. B - The Customer Identification Program (CIP) as part of AML compliance is designed to verify the identity of clients opening an account, crucial for preventing identity theft and financial fraud.

38. A - Providing a "Customer Relationship Summary" (Form CRS) helps retail investors understand the services offered and the fees charged, promoting transparency and informed decision-making.

39. B - The "Limit Order Display Rule" requires that broker-dealers display certain limit orders to the public, enhancing market transparency and the likelihood of order execution at favorable prices.

40. A - "Know Your Product" (KYP) requirements mandate that broker-dealers understand and effectively communicate the risks and rewards of the products they recommend, ensuring that recommendations are appropriate for their clients.

41. B - The "Order Protection Rule" ensures that trades are executed at the best available price, protecting investors from inferior execution prices and improving market efficiency.

42. B - The "Large Trader Reporting Rule" requires traders who conduct a substantial amount of trading activity to identify themselves to the SEC, facilitating oversight of market impact and activities.

43. B - FINRA's "Conflict of Interest Rule" requires firms to manage and disclose conflicts of interest, particularly those related to the allocation of investment opportunities among clients, ensuring fair treatment.

44. B - The "Market Access Rule" mandates that broker-dealers providing clients with access to the market maintain risk management controls to prevent erroneous orders and unauthorized trading, safeguarding the integrity of the markets.

MEMBER CONDUCT

1. C - The primary goal of establishing rules for member conduct within the securities industry is to protect investors and maintain fair, orderly, and efficient markets.

2. C - The Suitability Rule requires brokers to make recommendations that are suitable for their clients based on the client's financial situation and needs.

3. B - Churning refers to excessive trading in a client's account primarily to generate commissions, which is unethical and against regulatory standards.

4. C - The IPO Allocation Rule is designed to prevent conflicts of interest in the allocation of new issues, ensuring fair access to IPOs for all investors.

5. B - Front running is prohibited because it involves executing a broker's personal trades before client trades, exploiting confidential information for personal gain.

6. B - When opening a new account for a customer, brokers are required to verify the customer's identity and assess their investment profile under the Know Your Customer (KYC) rules.

7. B - The "Taping Rule" requires firms to record phone conversations to ensure compliance with trading and sales communications regulations, aiming to protect both the firm and its clients.

8. B - Regulation Best Interest (Reg BI) obligates brokers to act in the best interest of their retail customers when making a recommendation, elevating the standard of care.

9. D - A broker's failure to disclose material information to a client can be classified as misrepresentation or omission of facts, which is a serious breach of ethical and regulatory standards.

10. C - The prohibition against "selling away" is designed to prevent unauthorized transactions not supervised by the broker's firm, protecting investors from unsuitable or risky investments.

11. B - The purpose of Anti-Money Laundering (AML) compliance programs within brokerage firms is to detect and report potentially suspicious financial transactions, as part of efforts to combat money laundering and terrorism financing.

12. B - The requirement for firms to adopt a written Customer Identification Program (CIP) is part of the USA PATRIOT Act, aimed at preventing identity theft and financial fraud.

13. C - Marking the close is considered a manipulative or deceptive practice under securities law, as it involves artificially influencing the closing price of a security.

14. B - The duty to provide "best execution" for client trades means ensuring trades are executed in a timely manner and at the best available price, maximizing the value for clients.

15. B - The "Fair Dealing with Customers" principle requires securities professionals to ensure that all communications with customers are clear, fair, and not misleading, promoting transparency and trust.

16. B - The prohibition of "market manipulation" includes practices such as pump and dump schemes, which are designed to artificially inflate or deflate the price of securities for personal gain.

17. C - A broker's use of "discretionary authority" in a client's account without written authorization is a violation of FINRA rules, as it bypasses the client's control over their investment decisions.

18. B - The "Know Your Product" (KYP) requirement obligates brokers to understand the risks, rewards, and costs associated with the products they recommend, ensuring that recommendations are suitable and informed.

19. B - The SEC's "Order Protection Rule" aims to ensure that investors receive the best price execution for their orders, protecting against inferior execution prices in a fragmented market.

20. B - The practice of "wash trading" is prohibited as it creates a misleading appearance of market activity, manipulating the market for personal or institutional gain.

21. C - The "Customer Relationship Summary" (Form CRS) outlines the nature of the relationship between the broker-dealer and the retail investor, including fees, services, and conflicts of interest, enhancing transparency and informed decision-making.

22. B - The requirement for continuous and rigorous supervision of the trading activities of registered representatives is aimed at ensuring compliance with market regulations and protecting investor interests, maintaining the integrity of the securities market.

23. B - The primary purpose of a firm's compliance program is to monitor and enforce adherence to all applicable securities laws and regulations, ensuring the integrity of the financial markets and protecting investors.

24. B - An effective Anti-Money Laundering (AML) program must include procedures for detecting and reporting suspicious activities to help prevent money laundering and terrorism financing.

25. B - Regulation S-P requires firms to protect customers' privacy and safeguard their confidential information, ensuring that personal data is not misused or disclosed without authorization.

26. A - The Sarbanes-Oxley Act requires CEOs and CFOs to certify the accuracy of financial statements, enhancing the reliability of corporate disclosures and protecting investors.

27. A - Business Continuity Plans (BCP) are designed to ensure firms have a strategy for maintaining operations during significant disruptions, such as natural disasters or system failures, to minimize impact on clients and the market.

28. C - Cybersecurity regulations are designed to safeguard firms' and clients' digital information from unauthorized access or attacks, protecting against data breaches and cyber threats.

29. B - The "Know Your Customer" (KYC) rules are intended to verify the identity of clients and assess the suitability of investments, enhancing investor protection and preventing financial fraud.

30. A - Regulation Fair Disclosure (Reg FD) aims to ensure all investors have equal access to material company information, promoting fairness and transparency in the market.

31. B - The role of a firm's Chief Compliance Officer (CCO) is to oversee and enforce the firm's adherence to legal and regulatory compliance requirements, ensuring ethical and lawful operations.

32. B - Written Supervisory Procedures (WSP) manuals outline the supervisory structure and procedures for monitoring compliance with FINRA rules, essential for maintaining regulatory compliance and investor protection.

33. B - Periodic compliance training for employees is required to keep them informed about changes in securities laws and firm policies, ensuring that the firm's operations remain compliant with regulatory standards.

34. B - Restricted Lists are used by brokerage firms to prevent conflicts of interest by restricting trading in certain securities, particularly when the firm is involved in investment banking activities related to those securities.

35. B - The Office of the Whistleblower within the SEC encourages the reporting of securities law violations by offering protections and incentives, enhancing the detection and prosecution of securities fraud.

36. B - Due diligence on new products is required to verify that the products meet legal and regulatory standards and are suitable for clients, ensuring that investments are appropriate and in the best interest of clients.

37. B - The concept of "Material Nonpublic Information" (MNPI) is crucial in preventing insider trading, which involves trading based on confidential information not available to the general public.

38. B - The Consolidated Audit Trail (CAT) system is designed to provide a comprehensive database of all securities transactions to enhance market surveillance and regulatory oversight, improving the detection of market abuse and manipulation.

39. B - The requirement for firms to maintain accurate books and records under the Securities Exchange Act of 1934 facilitates the review and examination of a firm's business activities by regulators, ensuring transparency and accountability.

40. B - The "Customer Complaint Rule" requires firms to record and address all written complaints received from customers, ensuring that grievances are properly managed and resolved, and enhancing customer trust and satisfaction.

41. B - The practice of "marking the close" is prohibited because it involves manipulating the price of a security at the close of the market to benefit certain positions, undermining market integrity and fairness.

42. B - The "Net Capital Rule" is intended to ensure that broker-dealers maintain a cushion of liquidity sufficient to cover obligations to customers, protecting clients' assets and enhancing the financial stability of the securities industry.

43. B - Self-Regulatory Organizations (SROs) like FINRA regulate member brokerage firms and exchange markets to enforce federal securities laws, complementing the regulatory efforts of the SEC to maintain market integrity and protect investors.

44. B - The "Order Audit Trail System" (OATS) requirements help regulators track the lifecycle of orders to ensure market integrity and investigate potential violations, providing a detailed record of trading activity to detect and prevent market abuse.

COMPLIANCE CONSIDERATIONS

1. B - The primary goal of compliance programs within financial institutions is to monitor and enforce adherence to laws and regulations, ensuring ethical operations and protecting investors.

2. B - A key component of an Anti-Money Laundering (AML) compliance program is procedures for detecting and reporting suspicious activity, crucial for preventing financial crimes.

3. C - Regulation S-P is concerned with protecting customers' privacy and safeguarding their confidential information, a critical aspect of financial regulation.

4. C - Under the Sarbanes-Oxley Act, the CEO and CFO must certify the accuracy of financial reports, enhancing corporate accountability and transparency.

5. C - The purpose of a Business Continuity Plan (BCP) is to provide a strategy for the firm to continue operations under adverse conditions, ensuring resilience and continuity of service.

6. B - Cybersecurity regulations aim to protect against unauthorized access to digital information, safeguarding both the firm's and clients' data from cyber threats.

7. B - The "Know Your Customer" (KYC) rules are designed to verify the identity of clients and assess the suitability of investments, a foundational aspect of client relationship management.

8. B - Regulation Fair Disclosure (Reg FD) is intended to ensure all investors have equal access to material company information, promoting fairness and transparency in the market.

9. B - The Chief Compliance Officer (CCO) is responsible for enforcing adherence to legal and regulatory standards, a key role in maintaining the integrity of financial operations.

10. B - Written Supervisory Procedures (WSP) are required to outline the supervisory structure and procedures for compliance, ensuring a firm's operations align with regulatory expectations.

11. B - Periodic compliance training for employees is important because it keeps employees informed about regulatory changes and company policies, essential for maintaining compliance.

12. B - The use of Restricted Lists is primarily to prevent conflicts of interest by restricting trading in certain securities, protecting both the firm's and clients' interests.

13. B - The Office of the Whistleblower within the SEC was established to encourage reporting of securities law violations by offering protections and incentives, enhancing the enforcement of securities laws.

14. B - Due diligence on new products is necessary to verify that products meet legal and regulatory standards and are suitable for clients, ensuring responsible product offerings.

15. B - The concept of "Material Nonpublic Information" (MNPI) is crucial for preventing insider trading, a practice that undermines market fairness and investor trust.

16. B - The Consolidated Audit Trail (CAT) system was developed to provide a comprehensive database of securities transactions for market surveillance, enhancing regulatory oversight.

17. B - Maintaining accurate books and records is crucial for firms because it facilitates regulatory review and examination of the firm's business activities, ensuring transparency and accountability.

18. B - The "Customer Complaint Rule" mandates that firms record and address all written complaints received from customers, ensuring that grievances are properly managed and resolved.

19. C - "Marking the close" is prohibited because it involves manipulating the price of a security at the close of the market, a manipulative practice that distorts market integrity.

20. B - The "Net Capital Rule" ensures that broker-dealers maintain sufficient liquidity to meet obligations to customers, a critical requirement for financial stability and customer protection.

21. B - Self-Regulatory Organizations (SROs) like FINRA play a role in regulating member brokerage firms and exchange markets, complementing the regulatory framework established by federal securities laws.

22. B - The "Order Audit Trail System" (OATS) helps regulators track the lifecycle of orders to ensure market integrity, providing a vital tool for investigating and preventing market abuse.

23. B - Regulation S-P requires firms to adopt comprehensive policies and procedures to protect customer information from cybersecurity threats, ensuring the privacy and security of client data.

24. C - "Layering" or "spoofing" is considered a manipulative trading practice, where traders place orders with no intention of executing them to influence the price of securities.

25. B - To comply with the "Market Access Rule," firms must establish risk management controls and supervisory procedures to prevent erroneous orders and ensure market integrity.

26. C - The primary purpose of the Customer Identification Program (CIP) is to verify the identity of individuals opening accounts, as part of broader Anti-Money Laundering efforts.

27. B - Regulation BI (Best Interest) applies to recommendations made by broker-dealers to retail customers, ensuring that advisors act in the best interest of their clients.

28. B - The "Fiduciary Rule" primarily affects brokers and advisors providing retirement advice, requiring them to act in their clients' best interests.

29. C - FINRA Rule 4512 requires firms to keep accurate and updated customer account information, facilitating appropriate account management and compliance with regulatory requirements.

30. B - The SEC's "Regulation SCI" focuses on ensuring that technological systems of market participants are resilient, compliant, and capable of maintaining market integrity.

31. A - "Wash sales" are prohibited because they create artificial trading volume without actual change in ownership, misleading the market and other investors.

32. C - The primary objective of the "Patriot Act" in the financial industry is to prevent money laundering and terrorist financing, enhancing national security measures within financial transactions.

33. B - A "Chinese Wall" is intended to prevent the spread of confidential information across different areas of the firm, mitigating conflicts of interest and protecting sensitive data.

34. B - "Blue Sky Laws" are designed to protect investors from securities fraud at the state level, complementing federal securities regulations.

35. B - Under FINRA's Rule 2210, all communications with the public must be fair, balanced, and not misleading, ensuring that investors receive clear and accurate information.

36. B - The "Tick Size Pilot Program" was introduced to test the impact of wider tick sizes on small-cap stocks, assessing whether changes in tick size would improve market quality.

37. A - "Soft Dollars" practices involve the use of client brokerage commissions to purchase research and services, a practice that must be disclosed and managed to avoid conflicts of interest.

38. B - The "Volcker Rule" aims to prevent banks from making speculative investments that do not benefit their customers, reducing risks associated with such activities.

39. B - The "TRACE" system is used to report transactions in eligible fixed income securities, enhancing transparency and oversight in the bond market.

40. B - The "Global Investment Performance Standards" (GIPS) are ethical standards for presenting investment performance, promoting transparency and comparability in performance reporting.

41. A - The "Liquidity Coverage Ratio" (LCR) requirement under Basel III aims to ensure that banks have an adequate level of unencumbered high-quality liquid assets to withstand liquidity stress scenarios.

42. A - The "Fair Credit Reporting Act" (FCRA) is designed to ensure the accuracy and privacy of credit information, protecting consumers' rights in relation to their credit data.

43. B - "Regulation A+" allows companies to offer and sell securities up to a certain threshold without traditional registration, facilitating access to capital markets for smaller issuers.

44. B - The "Senior Safe Act" encourages financial professionals to report suspected cases of elder financial abuse without fear of liability, enhancing protections for senior investors.

A: Economic Fundamentals, Investment Strategies, and Market Dynamics

ECONOMIC INDICATORS

1. B - GDP measures the total market value of all goods and services produced within a country in a year, reflecting the size and health of its economy.

2. B - The Consumer Price Index (CPI) is an indicator of inflation or deflation, measuring changes in the price level of a market basket of consumer goods and services.

3. D - The Purchasing Managers' Index (PMI) is considered a leading indicator of economic health, reflecting the economic trends in the manufacturing and service sectors.

4. C - An increase in the Producer Price Index (PPI) typically indicates potential for increased inflation, as it measures the average changes in prices received by domestic producers for their output.

5. A - The unemployment rate measures the percentage of the total workforce that is unemployed and actively seeking employment, indicating the health of the labor market.

6. B - A yield curve inversion often indicates a potential recession, as it occurs when long-term debt instruments have a lower yield than short-term debt instruments.

7. C - The Federal Reserve might raise interest rates in response to signs of increasing inflation to temper economic growth and stabilize prices.

8. D - The balance of trade represents the difference between a country's exports and imports, indicating its economic relationship with the rest of the world.

9. D - Housing starts reflect the overall health of the real estate market and consumer confidence and spending power, as they indicate new residential construction activity.

10. A - Retail sales figures indicate trends in consumer spending, which is a major component of economic activity and an indicator of economic health.

11. A - Stagflation refers to an economy that is experiencing high inflation and high unemployment, a challenging scenario for economic policy.

12. C - Core CPI differs from CPI by excluding food and energy prices, providing a clearer view of long-term inflation trends without the volatility of these items.

13. C - A country's current account measures its trade balance, net income from abroad, and net current transfers, reflecting its financial relationship with the rest of the world.

14. C - An increase in consumer confidence typically leads to increased consumer spending, as individuals feel more secure about their financial situation.

15. B - The "Beige Book" provides a summary of economic conditions in each of the Federal Reserve's districts, offering insight into regional economic trends.

16. B - The Non-Farm Payroll report provides data on the number of jobs added or lost in the economy, excluding farm workers, and is a key indicator of economic health.

17. B - A country experiencing a trade deficit is importing more than it is exporting, which can have various implications for its economy.

18. B - The velocity of money refers to the rate at which money is exchanged in an economy, influencing inflation and economic activity.

19. B - The Labor Force Participation Rate measures the percentage of the working-age population that is part of the labor force, including both employed and unemployed individuals.

20. D - An increase in the Money Supply typically leads to lower interest rates and increased inflation as more money chases the same amount of goods and services.

21. A - The Capital to Labor Ratio is an indicator of the amount of capital allocated per labor unit in production, affecting productivity and economic growth.

22. A - Quantitative Easing is a monetary policy used to increase the money supply by purchasing government securities, aiming to stimulate economic growth by lowering interest rates.

23. B - The Producer Price Index (PPI) measures the average change in selling prices received by domestic producers for their output over time, indicating potential future consumer price inflation.

24. A - Real GDP refers to GDP adjusted for inflation, providing a more accurate measure of economic growth by accounting for changes in price levels.

25. C - A high Consumer Confidence Index indicates that consumers feel optimistic about the economy and are likely to spend more, potentially stimulating economic growth.

26. B - An increase in the Federal Funds Rate typically indicates that the Federal Reserve is trying to curb inflation by making borrowing more expensive.

27. D - The "Beige Book" is published eight times a year by the Federal Reserve, providing a qualitative review of economic conditions in each of its districts.

28. C - A persistent trade deficit may lead to the depletion of foreign reserves as a country spends more on imports than it earns from exports.

29. B - The Employment Cost Index (ECI) measures changes in the costs of employing labor, including wages and benefits, and is a key indicator of inflationary pressures in the labor market.

30. C - Quantitative easing involves the central bank purchasing assets to increase the money supply and encourage lending and investment, aiming to stimulate economic activity.

31. A - The National Debt is the total amount of money that a country's government has borrowed, not just the amount owed to foreign investors.

32. A - Inflation targeting refers to a policy where the central bank sets a specific inflation rate as its goal, using monetary policy tools to achieve it.

33. B - Leading Economic Indicators (LEI) are used to predict future economic activity, helping policymakers and investors anticipate changes in the economy.

34. A - The Phillips Curve illustrates the relationship between inflation and unemployment, suggesting a trade-off between the two in the short run.

35. C - Fiscal policy is determined by a government's budget decisions, including spending and taxation, affecting the economy's overall activity.

36. A - The money multiplier effect describes how an initial deposit can lead to a larger increase in the total money supply due to banks' ability to lend a portion of deposits.

37. C - Deflation is a condition in which prices for goods and services decrease, which can lead to decreased economic activity.

38. A - The discount rate is the interest rate charged to commercial banks on loans received from their regional Federal Reserve Bank, influencing the cost of borrowing money.

39. B - A budget surplus occurs when a government's revenues exceed its expenditures, indicating fiscal health.

40. B - The Gini coefficient is a measure of the distribution of income across a population, indicating the level of income inequality.

41. A - Crowding out refers to a situation where increased government spending leads to reduced investment by the private sector due to higher interest rates or other factors.

42. A - The Purchasing Power Parity (PPP) theory suggests that exchange rates should adjust to equalize the cost of a basket of goods in different countries, making the purchasing power equivalent.

43. C - Capital flight occurs when money rapidly leaves a country due to economic or political instability, often leading to a decrease in the value of the country's currency.

44. B - The "Twin Deficits" hypothesis relates to a country experiencing deficits in both its trade balance and government budget, suggesting that these deficits can be interrelated and may affect a country's economic health.

INVESTMENT STRATEGIES

1. B - Diversified investment strategy aims to reduce risk by spreading investments across various asset classes.

2. B - Value investing involves buying undervalued stocks in anticipation of their future growth.

3. B - Growth investing focuses on stocks expected to grow at an above-average rate compared to their industry.

4. B - Asset allocation is the process of dividing investments among different kinds of asset classes.

5. A - Dollar-cost averaging involves investing a fixed dollar amount into a particular investment on a regular schedule, regardless of the share price.

6. B - Passive management is employed by investors seeking to match the returns of a specific benchmark or index.

7. B - "Buy and hold" strategy is based on the belief that long-term investment offers the potential for significant returns, despite short-term market volatility.

8. B - The main focus of income investing is generating regular income from investments.

9. A - Sector rotation involves moving investments from one sector to another based on cyclical trends.

10. B - Market timing is attempting to predict market highs and lows to buy low and sell high.

11. C - A "contrarian" investment strategy involves going against prevailing market trends.

12. B - Technical analysis uses historical market data and charts to predict future price movements.

13. A - Risk parity is designed to allocate portfolio risk equally among different asset classes.

14. B - The "momentum" investment strategy is based on the idea that assets that have performed well will continue to do so.

15. A - Purchasing put options can protect against a potential decrease in the value of stock holdings.

16. B - ESG investing considers Environmental, Social, and Governance factors.

17. A - A hedge is a strategy used to limit or offset the probability of loss from price fluctuations.

18. A - The primary goal of portfolio rebalancing is to maintain a set level of risk over time.

19. A - Impact investing focuses on generating a financial return while also creating a positive social or environmental impact.

20. A - Short selling involves borrowing shares to sell at current prices, hoping to buy them back later at a lower price.

21. C - Fundamental analysis evaluates a company's financial health and prospects to determine its stock's intrinsic value.

22. D - An investor focusing on capital preservation is most likely to invest in Treasury securities and money market funds.

23. C - Income investing focuses on generating regular income, often through investments in companies that pay high dividends.

24. B - Socially responsible investing (SRI) focuses on investing in companies that meet certain ethical, social, and environmental criteria.

25. A - Currency hedging is used to protect against currency risk in international investments.

26. B - Leveraging refers to using borrowed money to increase the potential return of an investment.

27. B - Rebalancing a portfolio involves adjusting the proportions of different assets to maintain a desired asset allocation.

28. C - Day trading aims to benefit from short-term market movements.

29. C - An index fund is designed to replicate the performance of a specific market index.

30. C - The primary advantage of using a robo-advisor is lower costs and automated portfolio management based on algorithms.

31. B - Arbitrage involves taking advantage of price differences in different markets or forms for the same asset.

32. B - A balanced fund typically invests in a mix of stocks, bonds, and sometimes cash equivalents to provide both income and growth.

33. B - The goal of a "capital growth" investment strategy is to increase the value of the principal amount invested over time.

34. B - Strategic asset allocation refers to setting long-term asset mix targets and periodically rebalancing back to those targets.

35. B - The use of options in investment strategies can serve as a way to hedge against potential losses or to speculate on market movements.

36. A - "Value at risk" (VaR) is used to measure the maximum potential loss in an investment over a specific time period at a certain confidence level.

37. B - Investing in "emerging markets" is seen as a way to diversify a portfolio and potentially achieve higher returns, albeit with higher risk.

38. B - Dividend reinvestment plans (DRIPs) allow investors to automatically reinvest dividends to purchase additional shares of the stock.

39. A - The concept of "compounding" in investing refers to the process of accumulating interest on an investment, where the amount of interest earned itself earns interest over time.

40. B - A "defensive investment strategy" is primarily focused on reducing potential losses during market downturns.

41. B - "Smart beta" investing strategies aim to combine the benefits of passive and active investing to improve returns or reduce risk.

42. A - Real estate investment trusts (REITs) allow investors to invest directly in physical properties without owning them, offering a way to gain exposure to real estate.

43. B - Contractionary monetary policy aims to reduce inflation and slow economic growth by increasing interest rates.

44. C - Market capitalization refers to the total value of a company's outstanding shares of stock, representing the company's total market value.

MARKET DYNAMICS

1. D - Market liquidity refers to both the ease with which an asset can be converted into cash and the ability of a market to accept large transactions without impacting the price of the security.

2. B - Market volatility is the likelihood of rapid and significant price changes in a market.

3. A - Market depth is the extent to which a market can sustain large order sizes without affecting the price of the security.

4. A - The bid-ask spread is the difference between the highest price a buyer is willing to pay and the lowest price a seller is willing to accept.

5. B - A bull market is characterized by rising prices and optimism among investors.

6. B - A bear market is characterized by falling prices and pessimism among investors.

7. A - The efficient market hypothesis suggests that all known information is already reflected in stock prices.

8. B - High-frequency trading refers to the use of sophisticated algorithms to execute trades at very high speeds.

9. B - Market makers provide liquidity by always being ready to buy or sell at publicly quoted prices.

10. B - Short selling involves borrowing a stock to sell it with the intention of buying it back later at a lower price.

11. B - The primary function of the secondary market is to allow investors to buy and sell securities among themselves.

12. C - Price elasticity refers to how sensitive the price of a security is to changes in supply and demand.

13. B - Circuit breakers are designed to temporarily halt trading to curb panic-selling on days of extreme volatility.

14. B - Market sentiment is the overall attitude of investors toward a particular security or the market in general.

15. B - Portfolio diversification aims to reduce risk by spreading investments across various asset classes and sectors.

16. B - The primary market is where new securities are issued and sold for the first time.

17. A - An IPO refers to the process by which a private company becomes publicly traded by offering its shares to the public for the first time.

18. A - Market capitalization is calculated by multiplying the total number of a company's outstanding shares by the current market price of one share.

19. B - Liquidity risk refers to the risk associated with the inability to sell an investment at its current value.

20. A - Arbitrage is the practice of taking advantage of a price difference between two or more markets.

21. C - The term "overbought" suggests that a security is considered too expensive relative to its true value and might be due for a downturn.

22. C - A market correction is a short-term decline of 10% or more in the market or a security to adjust for overvaluation.

23. C - The primary function of a stock exchange is to facilitate the trading of securities.

24. A - A market order is an order to buy or sell a security at the current market price.

25. B - After-hours trading occurs before the regular market trading hours and after market close.

26. B - A limit order is an order to buy or sell a security at a specific price or better.

27. C - Market capitalization represents the total value of all outstanding shares of the company's stock.

28. B - Volume in market dynamics refers to the total number of shares or contracts traded in a security or market during a given period.

29. B - The bid price represents the price at which a buyer is willing to buy a security.

30. B - Market surveillance's primary purpose is to monitor trading activities for compliance with regulations and detect unusual trading patterns.

31. B - The primary purpose of a stock index is to measure the overall performance of a group of stocks.

32. C - When a stock or market index is "overvalued," it means it is trading at a price higher than its true value.

33. C - The "52-week high" and "52-week low" of a stock represent the highest and lowest prices the stock has traded at in the last 52 weeks.

34. C - A stock split is the process of issuing new shares to existing shareholders, increasing the number of shares outstanding.

35. A - Market sentiment refers to the collective mood of investors regarding the stock market.

36. B - The closing price of a security or index is the price at which it ends trading for the day.

37. B - The market capitalization of a company is calculated by multiplying the total number of outstanding shares by the current market price of one share.

38. B - The dividend yield of a stock is the annual income generated by a stock, expressed as a percentage of its current market price.

39. D - Market makers provide liquidity by always being ready to buy or sell at publicly quoted prices.

40. C - Short covering refers to the process of buying back borrowed shares to close out a short position.

41. B - A penny stock is a stock with a market price below $5 per share and is often characterized by high volatility.

42. C - Diversification aims to reduce risk by spreading investments across various asset classes and sectors.

43. B - Market manipulation involves deliberate actions to artificially inflate or deflate market prices or trading volumes.

44. B - The volatility index (VIX) measures the level of market uncertainty and expected price fluctuations.

CONCLUSION

In conclusion, "SIE Exam Prep 2024-2025" has equipped you with a solid foundation in securities industry essentials and effective test-taking strategies. We've emphasized the practical application of regulatory frameworks, bridged theory and practice, and provided tools for reinforcing your learning. As a bonus, the paperback version of the book includes a digital flashcards app to further enhance your study experience. Our mission is to inspire and empower you for success in the finance world. Remember, your journey continues, and the dynamic field of finance awaits your contributions. Best of luck on your SIE exam and in your future endeavors!

Made in United States
Orlando, FL
11 December 2024

55459045R00170